Development Theory

DEVELOPMENT THEORY

Four Critical Studies

Edited by

David Lehmann

FRANK CASS

First published 1979 in Great Britain by
FRANK CASS AND COMPANY LIMITED
Gainsborough House, Gainsborough Road,
London, E11 1RS, England

and in the United States of America by
FRANK CASS AND COMPANY LIMITED
c/o Biblio Distribution Centre
81 Adams Drive, P.O. Box 327, Totowa, N.J. 07511

ISBN 0 7146 3094 2 (Case)

ISBN 0 7146 4029 8 (Paper)

Printed in Great Britain by
The Bourne Press, 3–11 Spring Road, Bournemouth

Contents

Preface

Over the past few years the *Journal of Development Studies* has published several articles which, taken together, represent a substantial critique of the theories and approaches which pass for orthodoxy in the study of development and underdevelopment. We have therefore decided that these articles should be published together and the articles by Donal Cruise O'Brien and Wayne Nafziger, published first in 1972 and 1976, are reprinted in their original form. Dudley Seers has added a post-scriptum on the 'New Meaning of Development' to his 'Meaning of Development', published in 1972. Henry Bernstein, whose 'Modernization Theory and the Sociological Study of Development' dates from 1971, has written a completely new piece for this volume, which now presents a Marxist critique of both the 'conventional sociology of development' and the 'radical sociology of underdevelopment'.

DAVID LEHMANN

Introduction*

The essays published in this volume, taken together, constitute little less than an indictment of twenty or thirty years of theory and practice in the economics, sociology and politics of development. Or so it would appear. Further reflection would remind us that the indictment is almost exclusively directed at Anglo-Saxon theories, that those theories do have their defenders, but above all that the study of development is potentially one of the most creative areas in social science today, although, at the level of theory, that potential has still largely to be realized. The reasons for this can be sought in the relationship between 'development studies' and the development (or lack thereof) of social, economic and political theory in the period since the Second World War.

The mainstream concerns of development theory as described and criticized in these pages are not different in fundamental ways from the concerns of the 'founding fathers' of social science in the eighteenth and nineteenth centuries. Evolution, the division of labour, industrialism, class conflict and social cohesion, the conditions for the emergence of capitalism, the relations between state and civil society; the relations between theory and practice, and between the scholar and politics; and in economics, the 'optimum allocation of resources', the concept of comparative advantage and the theory of international trade, and the terms of trade between industry and agriculture. There are also echoes of nineteenth century Russian debates, between slavophiles and westernizers, between populists and marxists. This is hardly surprising, for the development of social science in the last century was in large part an effort to interpret the process of industrialization, and industrialization is a central concern of the study of development, even among its opponents. Whether this element of continuity between the traditions of social science and the theory of development testifies to sterility and stagnation, or to the abiding nature of the founding fathers' concerns is not clear, for other features of the relationship do testify to a questioning of or at least a departure from those same traditions—at least in the form in which they have been 'given and inherited' and passed on by modern sociology and economics. The ambiguities of the relationship are numerous, and we shall see that the 'critical' element in development studies can also be viewed as a reflection of criticisms of a purported orthodoxy which range across all the social sciences. It is merely unfortunate that what starts out as radical questioning tends so often to end up as a restatement, occasionally in ever-more-obscure language, of time-honoured formulations.

The study of development began in an era of optimism and growing prosperity for the advanced countries, and that climate is reflected in the

---

*I am grateful to John Toye for comments on an earlier draft.

1

subject's early concern for evolution and stability. Within a short space of time, however, it has fathered a radicalism which, in part at least, reflects the peculiar political involvement of social scientists in the political life of underdeveloped countries, as well as more general challenges to orthodox social theory—an orthodoxy which must rank as one of the shortest-lived in the history of social thought, having been removed from a position of hegemony to one of merely powerful influence in twenty years. It does not require an inordinately deep reading of the essays in this book to grasp a strong undercurrent of policy, or, better, political issues; it is difficult to believe that the authors would have been moved to make their analyses had they not felt at the time deep dissatisfaction with patterns of development they had observed, and had they not wished to discover a more egalitarian and autonomous pattern for the future. This concern and involvement which lie so close to the surface of writing on development problems are not a defect but a virtue, and are one (but only one) element which makes the subject so potentially creative. In advanced societies intellectuals rarely have easy access to the well-established policy-making machines, or to the closely knit networks of civil servants and *apparatchiki* and the politicians who are so heavily dependent upon them (Wildavsky and Heclo, 1974). Intellectuals are not, for those who occupy positions of power, a sensitive political group. In underdeveloped countries, in contrast, intellectuals are highly sensitive, and both local and foreign social scientists are taken seriously, if only to repress them; they may not ultimately have much independent influence on policies, but they do take part in the discussion of policy. Occasionally, as when they act as emissaries of some international institutions, their influence is substantial—for better or for worse. The involvement of social scientists in a far more 'wide open' arena than that available to them in the policy-making apparatuses of advanced countries, draws them into political and intellectual confrontations from which they are protected both in the groves of academe and in their forays into the predictable world of government administration and consultancy.

The opportunities and consequences are not unambiguous. The opportunity to 'advise a government' in a poor country may yield illusions of grandeur, resulting in the application of dogmatic models by professionals who are not willing to assume the responsibility for the political implications or preconditions of their advice. Evidently, governments choose advisers whom they find politically congenial, and to some extent whose advice they can safely predict, but this does not convert the adviser into an agent without responsibility. There are some quite frightening examples of technocrats' political ventriloquism: the prescription of draconian stabilization policies is an obvious example. The economic strategy followed by General Pinochet with the support and advice of Professors Harberger and Friedman and their pupils illustrates the thinness of the line between naivety and cynicism. Inverse examples are found in a progressive technocratism which advocates egalitarian policies in countries where the political conditions for their adoption are scarcely conceivable in the foreseeable future. Thus the ILO reports on employment to which Dudley Seers refers in his post-scriptum on the New Meaning of Development, and the pessimism of Clive Bell in his chapter on politics in the World Bank's *Redistribution with Growth* (Chenery et al. 1974). In Cuba, where 'progressives' might have found a more receptive audience, Charles Bettelheim, Ernest Mandel and, in a different vein, René Dumont, spoke to deaf ears—though there is some evidence that Dumont's *Is Cuba Socialist?*, vilified in public, was carefully noted in private.

The drawback of concern with policy is that it may attract attention away from wider theoretical issues insofar as it encourages research to concentrate on problems defined by national or international bureaucracies in terms of their definition of situations or their ideological or propagandistic requirements. (Note the dizzy succession of fashions which plagues the field: industrialization, employment, income distribution, basic needs etc. etc.) But it is not at all clear that exclusively theoretical reflection has yielded many returns either, as witness the inapplicability of ever more sophisticated planning models, or the arrested development which, as Henry Bernstein shows, has been the fate of 'dependency theory' (see also Leys, 1977). It is also instructive to return to Jonathan Levin's classic *Export Economies*, published in 1960, which says in a calm fashion, adducing a mass of Peruvian and Burmese evidence, most of what structuralists and *dependentistas* have subsequently said in more thunderous language.

Little work on development is today conducted outside university and national or international bureaucracies. The age of unbureaucratized but highly political dissidence is passed, but it is not clear that today's more 'professional' environment, which to some extent protects and legitimizes dissidence, produces better results. However strong his political inspiration, the social scientist working in a university or bureaucracy is inhibited from stating the political strategies entailed by the policies he or she produces. The political ventriloquism of the right is mirrored on the left. For example, it is asked how international institutions and banks could be persuaded to finance redistributive economic policies, and these institutions are heavily criticized for boycotting some left-wing governments; but a more realistic approach, based on harsh experience, to this question, would assume that these institutions (which finance so many intellectuals-cum-experts) will be at best indifferent to the pursuit of redistribution in all but very exceptional cases and that the international climate as a whole will be hostile. A second example concerns the internal implications of redistribution: frequently, redistribution, or its attempt, generates an inflation which threatens to reverse the entire process as well as provoke the overthrow of the government which impelled it; the use of rationing in order to prevent such a reversal requires a degree of centralization of economic control and of political mobilization rarely considered in policy blueprints. Beyond questions of strategy, the absence of political theory in the discussion of development is particularly noticeable. The experience of underdeveloped countries may cast doubt on the assumptions of Western social theory, but this is as nothing compared with the havoc it wreaks with the normative concepts which underlie our political institutions.

The study of development is not the most prestigious in the social science profession. Not infrequently it is confined to 'area studies' where interdisciplinarity, which has a low professional esteem, fails to achieve its promise. The results too often are 'undisciplinarity'. The institutional organization of social science contributes to the fossilization of theoretical models; this, plus the relegation of interdisciplinary work to a low status inhibits the cross-fertilization called for by development studies. The difficulty does not lie entirely at the level of disciplines, for the boundaries between them are ultimately founded upon models of social action and human behaviour, and barriers of communication between disciplines may well be underlain by barriers of communication between different theories. Interdisciplinary barriers do not appear insurmountable, for there are marxist sociologists and marxist economists, there are perfect competition models of politics as there are in economics. (Toye 1976). But the institutional organization of disciplines surely endows the bearers of orthodoxy with the power to deny respectability to critical activity and thus confines it to the institutional underworld of dissidence where, concentrating its energies on tasks of destruction, its growth is stunted. Meanwhile, the study of development is in danger of becoming a ghetto in which embattled ideologies pursue their mutual destruction without offering any prospect of the proclaimed 'new synthesis'.

The authors of the theories criticized in these essays are not prominent students of the development process, but rather prominent social scientists who have conducted 'forays' into the field. Few of them have conducted any sustained empirical research in a poor country. Modernization theories are adaptations of a specific reading—Talcott Parsons' reading expounded in his *Structure of Social Action*—of Weber and Durkheim. One writer who places himself in that same school and yet has made a major contribution to the understanding of social processes in an under-developed country is Fred Riggs, who spent many years in South-East Asia. Riggs' remarkably perceptive ethnography of bureaucratic and political power (see Cruise O'Brien's essay) survives even his own attempts to force his interpretation into a structural-functional framework by using the terminology of optics (see the first hundred pages of *Administration in Developing Countries: the Theory of Prismatic Society*.) A similar exception is Robin Luckham's study of the *Nigerian Military*, which stands out among studies emerging from the model of professionalization first developed and later propagated by Morris Janowitz. Luckham's dissatisfaction with that approach has since led him to develop a marxist theory for the study of the military and the international weapons trade (Luckham, 1977).

Among marxists the divorce between theoretical development and empirical research is no less observable. Established in opposition to an orthodoxy which may reflect the prejudices and interests of the powerful but has had little ultimate intellectual success, the modern marxist critique has attracted many adherents as a critique; but as the basis for empirical investigation or of policy it has yet to yield results.

The empirical work which most inspires marxist critiques is that of historians such as Barrington Moore, Eric Hobsbawm and Perry Anderson, or that of non-marxist, though also non-neo-classical, economists who have laid bare the operations of multinational corporations (Vaitsos, 1973; Vernon, 1973), or who have undertaken detailed work on the relationship between income distribution and growth (Fishlow, 1972; Bacha and Taylor, 1978; Kuznets, 1955). In policy, marxists have recourse to the Soviet industrialization debate, which may be considered the first modern debate on development policy (Erlich, 1960; Lewin, 1968; Preobrazhensky, 1965) or to current Chinese experience (Paine, 1976) expressed in a language far removed from the abstractions of *dependencia* or the conceptualization of modes of production (Hindess and Hirst, 1975). The Soviet debate, which finds later incarnations in Indian debates about the relations between agriculture and industry (Byres, 1974; Lipton, 1977;

Mitra, 1977) is certainly one of the most fruitful in development studies, and one of the rare cases in which a marxist approach to the formulation of questions casts more light on policy-makers' problems than do other approaches (see my review of Lipton, which tries to show that urban-rural relations are better formulated in marxist terms than in neo-classical ones, Lehmann, 1977).

Returning to the level of theory, it is possible that the polemics in development studies are reflections of arguments being conducted in the social sciences as a whole. It is not correct to claim that the various orthodoxies are challengeable only because they are 'inapplicable' to underdeveloped countries. There may be many other reasons. If it turns out that what is wrong is the general social or economic theory on which theories of modernization or economic development are founded, then the theory of development becomes an academic issue. One might therefore ask whether the study of society and economy in underdeveloped countries requires or can produce a theoretical apparatus with the following characteristics:

(a) which provides a comprehensive framework for the analysis of social processes resulting from the incorporation of new territories, societies and polities into the world economic and political system, and
(b) which includes enough variables on which to base explanations of variations observed in this process of incorporation.

It is surely enough merely to state this agenda in order to realize that any theory of development which is neither teleological nor functionalist is highly unlikely to succeed. It is therefore hardly surprising to note the strong element of teleology in many theories of development, even in those which profess an opposition to teleology and functionalism. One must distinguish, as Henry Bernstein does, implicitly, between the hitherto unfruitful theories of development and theories applied to the study of social and economic structures of underdeveloped countries. It is in the attempt to draw from the tradition of social science (as interpreted by Parsons) a theory applicable to the Third World as a whole and to the totality of social processes within it that failure has been most evident. More limited—but nevertheless ambitious—enterprises, such as those of Barrington Moore and Perry Anderson, who confine themselves to class relations and politics, turn out to be firmly in the traditions of Marx and Weber, to find favour with the critics of orthodoxy and to lack that aspiration to the infinite which characterized the theory of modernization. One may therefore wonder whether the limits of development theory have lain in the globality of its project rather than in its theoretical origins.

The creative potential of development studies arises precisely from those features thereof which I have discussed and on whose dangers I have insisted perhaps too much: the inescapable political involvement, the difficulty of confining an analysis to one particular discipline, and the possibility it offers of comparative study and of extracting generalizations therefrom. The theories criticized in this volume relied on a comparison of today's advanced countries and their history with the social and economic structure of underdeveloped countries, but in the future we may see more and more comparative study between different countries and regions of the Third World, thus enriching the subject substantially.

What, then, might the 'crisis' in the development studies, if it exists, consist of? At the level of pure theory it would be the product of a more general crisis of the social sciences. If by 'crisis' is meant simply a situation in which dominant theories are being challenged, then this is a healthy situation, and not such a rare one. We assume all too easily that, before the mid-sixties, there was a period of calm in which structural-functional sociology and neo-classical economics occupied a hegemonic position. Perhaps, but if so it was a short period, and although structural-functionalism may have been hegemonic in the United States, it never penetrated the great walls of English empiricism. The symptoms of crisis should rather be seen in the failure of self-styled critical, radical and alternative approaches to generate a new theoretical apparatus, and in the possible absence of suitable conditions for the production of such an alternative; for the projected alternatives occasionally bear uncanny resemblances to theories which have gone before: thus the parallels between Althusserian marxism and functionalism itself, both of which interpret social phenomena in terms of their contribution to the maintenance of 'the system'—a word, which like so many key words in social science, can sound nice or nasty depending on the context in which it is uttered.

REFERENCES

Perry Anderson: *Passages from Antiquity to Feudalism,* London, New Left Books, 1974.
Perry Anderson: *Lineages of the Absolutist State,* London, New Left Books, 1974.
Edmar Bacha and Lance Taylor: "Brazilian Income Distribution in the 1960's: Model Results and the Controversy", *Journal of Development Studies,* XIV, 3, April 1978.
T. J. Byres: "Land Reform, Industrialization and the Marketed Surplus in India: an essay in Rural Bias", in David Lehmann (ed.): *Agrarian Reform and Agrarian Reformism,* London, Faber and Faber, 1974.
Hollis Chenery et al.: *Redistribution with Growth,* London, Oxford University Press, 1974.
René Dumont: *Cuba, est-il Socialiste?,* Paris, Seuil, 1970.
Alexander Erlich: *The Soviet Industrialization Debate,* Cambridge, Mass., Harvard University Press, 1960
Barry Hindess and Paul A. Hirst: *Pre-capitalist Modes of Production,* London, Routledge and Kegan Paul, 1975.
Simon Kuznets: "Economic Growth and Income Inequality", *American Economic Review,* XLV, March 1955.
Albert Fishlow: "Brazilian Size Distribution of Income", *American Economic Review,* LXII, pp. 391–402, May 1972.
David Lehmann: "Neo-classical Populism", *Peasant Studies,* VI, 4, October 1977.
Moshe Lewin: *Russian Peasants and Soviet Power,* London, Allen and Unwin, 1968.
Jonathan Levin: *The Export Economies,* Cambridge, Mass., Harvard University Press, 1960.
Colin Leys: "Underdevelopment and Dependency: Critical Notes", *Journal of Contemporary Asia,* VII, 1, 1977.
Michael Lipton: *Why Poor People Stay Poor: Urban Bias in World Development,* London, Temple Smith, 1977
Robin Luckham: *The Nigerian Military,* London, Cambridge University Press, 1971.
Robin Luckham: "Militarism: Force, Class and International Conflict", *Bulletin* of the Institute of Development Studies, IX, 1, July 1977.
Robin Luckham: "Militarism: Arms and the Internationalisation of Capital", *ibid.* VII, 3, March 1977.
Ashok Mitra: *Terms of Trade and Class Relations,* London, Frank Cass, 1977.
Barrington Moore Jr.: *The Social Origins of Dictatorship and Democracy,* Boston, Beacon Press, 1967.

Suzanne Paine: "Balanced Development: Maoist Theory and Chinese Practise", *World Development,* April 1976.

Talcott Parsons: *The Structure of Social Action,* Glencoe, The Free Press, 1949.

E. Preobrazhensky: *The New Economics,* London, Oxford University Press, 1965.

Fred Riggs: *Administration in Developing Countries: the Theory of Prismatic Society* Boston, Houghton Mifflin, 1964.

John Toye: "Economic Theories of Politics and Public Finance", *British Journal of Political Science,* VI, pp. 433–447, October 1976.

Constantin Vaitsos: *Intercountry Income Distribution and the Transfer of Technology* London, Oxford University Press, 1973.

Raymond Vernon: *Sovereignty at Bay,* Harmondsworth, Penguin, 1973.

Aaron Wildavsky and Hugh Heclo: *The Private Government of Public Money,* London Faber and Faber, 1974.

The Meaning of Development

Dudley Seers*

Why do we confuse development with economic growth? Surely one could hardly say that the situation depicted by a set of projections was preferable to that shown by another set simply because the former implied higher *per capita* income. After all, in what sense is South Africa more developed than Ghana, or Kuwait than the U.A.R., or the United States than Sweden?

One explanation is that the national income is a very convenient indicator. Politicians find a single comprehensive measure useful, especially one that is at least a year out of date. Economists are provided with a variable which can be quantified and movements in which can be analysed into changes in sectoral output, factor shares or categories of expenditure, making model-building feasible.

We can, of course, fall back on the supposition that increases in national income, if they are sufficiently fast, sooner or later lead to the solution of social and political problems. But the experience of the past decade makes this belief look rather naïve. Social crises and political upheavals have emerged in countries at all stages of development. Moreover, we can see that these afflict countries with rapidly rising *per capita* incomes, as well as those with stagnant economies. In fact it looks as if economic growth not merely may fail to solve social and political difficulties; certain types of growth can actually cause them.

Now that the complexity of development problems is becoming increasingly obvious, this continued addiction to the use of a single aggregative

* Director of the Institute of Development Studies at the University of Sussex. The first third of this paper is derived from 'The meaning of development' published in the *International Development Review* (Vol. 11, No. 4, 1969), and republished in I.D.S. Communications Series, No. 44; *Revista Brasileira de Economia*, (Vol. 24, No. 3); *Internationale Spectator*, (Vol. XXIV, No. 21); *Ekistics*, 1970; *Sociological Abstracts*, U.S.A., 1970; *The Political Economy of Development* (ed. Ilchman and Uphoff) 1971; and *INSIGHT*, July 1971. I am grateful for comments from Hans Singer on a draft of this part, which was also discussed at seminars at the Universities of Boston and Toronto, and formed the basis of a lunch talk at the 11th World Conference of the Society for International Development (New Delhi, November 1969). The remainder was written specially for this collection.

indicator, in the face of the evidence, takes on a rather different appearance. It begins to look like a preference for avoiding the real problems of development.

THE DEFINITION OF DEVELOPMENT

In discussing the challenges we now face, we have to dispel the fog around the word 'development' and decide more precisely what we mean by it. Only then will we be able to devise meaningful targets or indicators, and thus to help improve policy, national or international.

The starting-point is that we cannot avoid what the positivists disparagingly refer to as 'value judgements'. 'Development' is inevitably a normative concept, almost a synonym for improvement. To pretend otherwise is just to hide one's value judgements.

But from where are these judgements to come? The conventional answer, which Tingerben accepts for his system of economic planning, is to draw our values from governments. But governments have necessarily a rather short-term view, in some cases discounting the future at a very high rate. More seriously, some governments are themselves the main obstacles to development, on any plausible definition, and once this is conceded, where is one to obtain the yardsticks by which government objectives are to be judged? Even supposing that governments represented faithfully, in some sense, popular attitudes, these are endogenous to the development process and therefore cannot provide a means of assessing it.

Another approach is to copy the development paths of other countries, which implicitly means aiming at thir present state as the goal. This is what model-builders, for example, are really doing when coefficients are taken from an international cross-section analysis, or from functions that fit the experience of an industrial country. Yet few if any of the rich countries now appear to the outside world as really desirable models. Some aspects, such as their consumption levels, seem enviable, but these are associated, perhaps inseparably, with evils such as urban sprawl, advertising pressures, air pollution and chronic tension. Besides it is by no means obvious or even likely that the rest of the world could trace the history of the industrial countries even if they wanted to.

If values are not to be found in politics or history, does this mean that we are each left to adopt our own personal set of values? This is fortunately not necessary. Surely the values we need are staring us in the face, as soon as we ask ourselves: what are the necessary conditions for a universally acceptable aim, the realization of the potential of human personality?

If we ask what is an *absolute* necessity for this, one answer is obvious—enough food. Below certain levels of nutrition, a man lacks not merely bodily energy and good health but even interest in much besides food. He cannot rise significantly above an animal existence. If anyone has any doubt on the primacy of food, they should reflect on the implications of recent research [*Scrimshaw and Gordon, 1968*] showing that if young children are not properly nourished the result may well be lasting impairment not merely of the body, but also of the mind.

Since foodstuffs have prices, in any country the criterion can be expressed in terms of income levels. This enables it to take account also of certain other minimum requirements. People never spend all their money (or energy) on food, however poor they are. To be enough to feed a man, his income has also to cover basic needs of clothing, footwear and shelter.

But I am not talking about consumption needs in general; I am talking about the capacity to buy physical necessities.

Peter Townsend and others who support a 'relative' concept of poverty describe those in any society as poor if they are unable to 'participate in the activities and have the living conditions and amenities which are customary in that society. These activities and customs have to be described empirically. In addition to food and clothing customs, they include, for example, in the United Kingdom, such things as birthday parties for children, summer holidays and evenings out' [Townsend, 1970, p. 42]. This concept of poverty as social deprivation implies that the poverty standard would rise as living conditions improve, and indeed that poverty could *never* be eliminated, except perhaps by making the distribution of income very equal. But to see one's child doomed by malnutrition to life-long physical and mental inferiority or to be unable to buy a blood transfusion to save one's wife's life is surely a different sort of poverty from being unable to afford the cakes for a children's party or to take one's wife out to the pictures.

What I am asserting is that below the level at which a man can in some sense provide 'enough' food for his family, the marginal utility of income is much greater than it is above that level. This is of course an old-fashioned view, and it raises many problems of concepts and measurement to which I return later. But wherever there is serious poverty, a normative approach to development, which I have argued to be inevitable, implies a utility function of this general shape.

Another basic necessity, in the sense of something without which personality cannot develop, is *a job*. This does not necessarily mean paid employment: it can include studying, working on a family farm or keeping house. But to play none of these accepted roles, i.e. to be chronically dependent on another person's productive capacity, even for food, is incompatible with self-respect for a non-senile adult, especially somebody who has been spending years at school, perhaps at university, preparing for an economically active life.

It is true, of course, that both poverty and unemployment are associated in various ways with income. But even a fast increase in *per capita* income is in itself far from enough, as the experience of many economies shows, to reduce either poverty or unemployment. In fact, certain processes of growth can easily be accompanied by, and in a sense cause, growing unemployment.[1]

The direct link between *per capita* income and the numbers living in poverty is *income distribution*. It is a truism that poverty will be eliminated much more rapidly if any given rate of economic growth is accompanied by a declining concentration of incomes. Equality should, however, in my belief, be considered an objective in its own right, the third element in development. Inequalities to be found today, especially in the Third World where there is massive poverty, are objectionable by any religious or ethical standards. The social barriers and inhibitions of an unequal society distort the personalities of those with high incomes no less than of those who are poor. Trivial differences of accent, language, dress, customs, etc., acquire an absurd importance and contempt is engendered for those who lack social graces, especially country dwellers. Since race is usually highly correlated with income, economic inequality lies at the heart of racial tensions. More seriously, inequality of income is associated with other inequalities, especially in education and political power, which reinforce it.

The questions to ask about a country's development are therefore: What has been happening to poverty? What has been happening to unemployment? What has been happening to inequality? If all three of these have become less severe, then beyond doubt this has been a period of development for the country concerned. If one or two of these central problems have been growing worse, especially if all three have, it would be strange to call the result 'development', even if *per capita* income had soared. This applies, of course, to the future too. A 'plan' which conveys no targets for reducing poverty, unemployment and inequality can hardly be considered a 'development plan'.[2]

Of course, the true fulfilment of human potential requires much that cannot be specified in these terms. I cannot spell out all the other requirements, but this paper would be very unbalanced if I did not mention them at all. They include adequate educational levels (especially literacy), participation in government and belonging to a nation that is truly independent, both economically and politically, in the sense that the views of other governments do not largely predetermine one's own government's decisions.[3]

As undernourishment, unemployment and inequality dwindle, these educational and political aims become increasingly important objectives of development. Later still, freedom from repressive sexual codes, from noise and pollution, become major aims.[4] But these would not override the basic economic priorities, at least for really poor countries, with large numbers of undernourished children. A government could hardly claim to be 'developing' a country *just because* its educational system was being expanded or political order was being established, or limits set on engine noise, if hunger, unemployment and inequality were significant and growing, or even if they were not diminishing. Indeed, one would doubt the viability of political order in these circumstances, if one didn't consider the claim *prima facie* somewhat suspect; on the other hand, certain political patterns may well be incompatible with development.

Before leaving this issue I must make it clear that the national income is not totally meaningless, just because it is an inappropriate indicator of development. It has some significance as a measure of development *potential*. Suppose that two countries start a decade with the same *per capita* income and one grows faster than the other over ten years, but that the increase in income in the former goes entirely to the rich, and that, because growth has been due to highly capital-intensive techniques, unemployment rates remain unchanged, while in the latter growth has been slower but has meant lower unemployment and thus benefited the poorest class. Then, although the country with faster growth has, on my criteria, developed least—in fact not developed at all—it has achieved greater potential for developing later.

In the first place, the fiscal system could bring about development more rapidly the greater the income available for transfer to the poor. Moreover, a fast growth rate implies a greater savings capacity, which could more easily mean true development in the future. Indeed the faster-growing country may well already have a higher level of investment *per capita*;

if this investment is in agricultural projects which will raise food production and provide more rural employment, or in rural schools, genuine development could already be foreshadowed for the future.[5]

From a long-term viewpoint, economic growth is for a poor country a necessary condition of reducing poverty. But it is not a sufficient condition. To release the development potential of a high rate of economic growth depends on policy. A country where economic growth is slow or negligible may be busy reshaping its political institutions so that, when growth comes, it will mean development; such a country could develop faster in the long run than one at present enjoying fast growth but with political power remaining very firmly in the hands of a rich minority. It will be interesting to compare, for example, what happens in Cuba and Brazil in the remainder of this century.

PRIORITIES IN THE SOCIAL SCIENCES

It may help us to withstand the strong intellectual attraction of the national income as a yardstick of development if we look back a little.

By about 1950 the great economic problems had been brought largely under control in the industrial countries. Unemployment had been reduced to historically very low levels; absolute poverty in the sense I use the word had been largely eliminated; taxation and educational advances had reduced economic inequalities, and, though a good deal of what remained was associated with race, this was not a source of great political at that time, and it was largely overlooked by the social scientists, especially the economists.

We could say that these countries had managed in various ways to meet, in some degree at least, the challenges they had faced in the 19th century. One reason, of course, was that they benefited from world economic leadership and political power—to this I'll return later. But another was that social scientists such as Booth, Towntree, Boyd-Orr, the Webbs, Keynes, Beveridge and Tawney focused attention sharply on poverty, unemployment and inequality in the first half of this century. (I hope I am not being excessively nationalistic in choosing British examples: the names *are* rather significant.) Most economists, even Pigou, took greater equality as an obviously desirable objective.

With the easing of the big problems, however, economists turned their attention to innovations in professional techniques. In as far as they retained interest in current affairs, it was mainly in the progress of the nation conceived as a whole. The national income seemed ideal for comparing growth rates of a country during different periods, or for constructing an international league table. Moreover, it has maintained its role as a predictor of the level of employment—if the economy is diversified and the labour force is mobile, big short term changes in the national income are closely associated with changes in employment.[6]

We now see that even in the industrial countries basic economic problems had not really been cured. Their social scientists, notably in the United States, have been rediscovering their own poverty. Moreover, unemployment has recently grown, and inequality may well have done so too.

But the fundamental problems have never even started to disappear from sight in the Third World. In Africa, Asia or Latin America, development had been very limited on any of the three economic criteria until

1950. Since then, there has certainly been some reduction in the proportion, even if not in absolute numbers, living in poverty. But it has recently been estimated by Francis Keppel that seven out of every ten children in the entire world are 'affected by the apathy typical of chronic protein deficiency, an apathy which translates into diminished learning potential' [*Scrimshaw and Gordon, 1968*]; the fraction among many countries of the Third World, such as India, must of course be higher. Unemployment seems to have grown, judging from the countries for which data are available. It is probable, though data are extremely poor, that in most countries inequality has not been reduced; in many, it may well have increased. A paper by A. J. Jaffe [*1969*] on five Latin American countries for which comparable studies over time are available concludes that all showed increasing inequalities, with the possible exception of Mexico. It is even possible that, were the data available, we would find economic growth to be directly associated with growing unemployment and increasing inequality. If that has indeed been the case, there has been a negative correlation between growth and development. Even if that were not so, it is clear that the connection between them is not at all as straightforward as was once believed.

CONCEPTUAL AND MEASUREMENT PROBLEMS

One defence of the *national income* is that it is an objective, value-free indicator, Yet it is in fact heavily value-loaded: every type of product and service is assigned its own particular weight (many being zero). This weight is mainly determined by market forces, which reflect the country's income distribution. A familiar question in economics—how adequately income measures demand when its distribution is unequal—gets additional point when the distribution is as highly concentrated as it is in the countries of the Third World. Another question—how objective demand is when it is partially determined by salesmanship—appears even more cogent when tastes are to some extent imported from abroad. But, in addition, official policies, e.g. fostering import substitution by controls, often increase the prices of luxuries much more than of necessities. There are often egalitarian reasons for such policies, but the outcome is paradoxically that increases in production of luxuries count very much more highly in the estimation of rates of economic growth than they do in industrial countries.[7] While prices of staple foods and clothing may be comparable between poor countries and rich, perhaps lower in the former, prices of cars, refrigerators, etc., are several times as high. The absurd consequence may be that in a country where there is serious poverty, a car counts for more than ten tons of rice.

To estimate or use the national income also implies a set of judgements about what activities it should cover—what are the 'final' products, as against 'intermediate' products which are not considered intrinsically valuable and only produced because they make possible the products of other, more desirable, products. This raises the basic question: what activities are we trying to maximize?—a question once posed by Kuznets and now revived by Sametz [*1968*].[8] The issue of distribution can be raised in these terms too—are the luxuries of the professional classes a 'necessary cost' of raising the incomes of the poor, the real maximand?

It has also been argued on behalf of national income as a development

indicator that it could at least be quantified. But what are all the volumin-
ous tables of national income accounts really worth? So far as the Third
World is concerned, much of what they ought to cover is virtually outside
the scope of official statistics. This applies above all to output of domestic
foodstuffs, even the staples, let alone subsidiary crops which come under
the general heading of 'market gardening' (American 'truck farming'),
not to speak of fish, forest products, etc. Extremely rough methods of
estimation are often used, much of the output being assumed to rise in
proportion to the increase in rural population, an increase which is in
turn assumed to be some constant arbitrary rate in the absence of regis-
tration of births and deaths, or data on migration.[9] Secondly, we know
very little about construction in the countryside by the farming community
itself; this apparently amounts to a good deal if one takes account not
only of building houses, but also clearing land, digging wells and ditches,
constructing fences and hedges, etc. Thirdly, there are practically no basic
data on domestic service and other personal services, even those which are
remunerated.

We should ask national income estimators conceptual questions such
as: which of the activities a farm family does for itself without payment,
such as haircutting for example, have you included in the national income?
And why? And practical questions such as: how many fishes were caught
in Province A in the years concerned? How many huts were constructed in
Province B? How many barbers worked in Province C? And how do
you know?

We should also ask those who quote the national income, for example
in a planning office or a university, how much time they have spent with
the estimators? It is unsafe and therefore unprofessional to use national
income data until one has personally satisfied oneself on how such questions have been handled.

I have examined the worksheets in about twenty countries; the blunt
truth of the matter is that when one takes into account the difficulties of
allowing for inventory changes and depreciation, and of deflating current-
price data, the published national income series for a large number of
countries have very little relevance to economic reality.[10] In many countries, any reasonably competent statistician could produce from the mea-
gre basic data series showing the real *per capita* income either rising or
falling. Decimal places are fantasy. Some series are in fact in a way more
misleading than sets of random numbers would be, because they *appear*
to have a significance. It would, of course, be very convenient if the national income data published in such quantities had objective meaning,
but unfortunately this does not make them meaningful.

It might be argued that some numbers called national income series
are at least available, whereas data on poverty, unemployment and inequality are very scrappy. This is, however, the result not so much of basic
differences in estimation possibilities as of attitudes to development. The
type of data collected reflects priorities. What work is done by a statistical
office depends in practice partly on what its own government demands,
partly on the advice it receives from various U.N. agencies, especially
the U.N. Statistical Office. As a realization of the importance of social
problems spreads, statistical offices will put less weight on national income estimation, more on preparing appropriate social indicators.[11]

I do not deny that there are conceptual problems with development

indicators too. The difficulties in assessing *poverty* standards, or even minimum nutritional standards, are well known.[12] For a household these
should reflect the ages and also the physical activities of its members.[13]
Moreover, many households which can afford to exceed the nutritional
minimum expenditure will not in fact do so, because they spend their money in a sense unwisely (whether because of conventional expenditures on
non-essentials, lack of information or personal taste).[14] The recognition
of this is indeed implicit in the official U.S. poverty line which allows
$750 a head, of which about $250 is for food.

But we need not give up. When as in India, an official poverty line
has been established, the resultant estimates of the proportion with incomes
below a specified poverty line are not without meaning.[15] However rough,
they have some significance as a yardstick for measuring development
over time—certainly such comparisons convey more than changes in the
per capita national income.

There are other well-known measures of poverty which I can only mention briefly here. One is the infant mortality rate (though this reflects in
particular the effectiveness of health services, as well as diet, housing, etc.).
Data on protein consumption and the incidence of diseases of undernourishment, such as rickets, are further clues on development, as are the
height and weight of children.[16] However, they are only clues, and may
well be misleading if used to compare nations of very different genetic
stock, dietary habits, etc.

Unemployment is, of course, notoriously difficult to define in non-
industrial societies. An urban unemployed person can be roughly identified by the usual test questions designed to reveal the last occasion when
work was sought (though this means excluding from the unemployed
those who would only look for a job if they thought there was any chance
of finding it, and on the other hand including those who would in fact
only accept particular types of work). In addition there is involuntary
short time working, and people are more or less idle, at least for most of
the day, in jobs which are more or less fictional (from superfluous posts in
government to shining shoes). The volume of this is hard to measure; so is
disguised rural under-employment because of seasonal variations in
activity. One needs much more detail by sector, by region, by sex, by age,
by educational qualification, to throw light on the nature of unemployment and underemployment in any country and on the attitudes of people
to work.[17]

Inequality can be measured in many ways—by size, race, region, or by
factor shares. All have their uses for different purposes, and they are of
course all interconnected. They are also all limited in one important respect, namely that there are other sources of inequality than income. One's
standard of living may be affected by access to free cars, for example. (An
ambassador may well have a higher level of living than somebody with ten
times his salary.) It also depends on access to public services such as health
(especially important in urban-rural comparisons). More fundamentally,
political power may greatly influence the inequality of people in terms of
their ability to develop their personality, even to speak their minds.

Even concentration of income by size can be measured in many ways.
If one wants a single measure, the Gini coefficient, derived from the Lorenz
curve (showing cumulative proportions of income received by cumulative
proportions of recipients), is probably still the most useful, for either in-

come or wealth. But, if we are mainly concerned with inequality as a cause of poverty, a more meaningful measure may be to express (say) the lowest decile as a fraction of the median (following the general approach in a recent study by Harold Lydall [*1968*].[18] We are after all not greatly interested in changes *within* the top half of the income ladder.

Of course, all these measures of distribution raise the same conceptual problems as national income measurement—for example, where to draw the boundary between activities which are marketed and those which are not. In addition, such measures take no account of the price structure, which may well affect the concentration of *real* income—an important point in, e.g., countries where the burden of protection is borne mainly by the rich.

All in all, however, the conceptual problems of these indicators do not seem to be more formidable than those of the national income—we have just grown accustomed to ignoring the latter. And many of the practical problems are the same as those that face the national income estimators. But indicators of any of the elements of development I have mentioned also require supplementary information. Thus to measure the proportion of the population above a poverty line one needs to know how many people share each household income (and whether they are males or females, adults or children). To measure unemployment meaningfully, one needs to know what jobs people would be prepared to take (and at what income), and what hours they work. To measure distribution in any of its dimensions, one needs to know more than the national estimator about who receives various types of income.

But again we must not be diverted by such technical problems from attempting the assessment which really matters. There is one possible source for all of these measures, surveys of households designed to provide them; these can yield the necessary cross-classifications by region, race, income, etc. The systematic development of the information required to study trends in poverty, unemployment and income distribution in any country requires pilot surveys in depth to clarify the conceptual issues in their local context and guide the construction of indicators. This is best achieved if a permanent sampling organization, such as India has in its National Sample Survey, is established to collect the necessary information professionally, systematically and regularly.

I can only mention briefly indicators for the educational and political dimensions of development. In as far as education is provided by the formal educational system (which is very much open to argument) the main source is, of course, inputs and outputs of various levels of education. A technique for combining these in a diagram showing trends over time has been developed by Richard Jolly [*1969*].

Measurement of the extent to which the political aims have been achieved is of course much more difficult; possible clues include the number of prisoners held for political or quasi-political reasons, and the social and racial composition of parliaments, business boards, senior public administrative grades, etc., and also of those enjoying secondary and university education.

More general indicators of welfare, reflecting political and other influences, include the rates per million people of crimes of violence, suicide, alcoholism and other types of drug addiction. Here the main problem is to cope with the consequences of different standards of reporting, stemming from differences in definition (what is an alcoholic?) and in coverage (e.g. comprehensiveness of police records, death registers, etc.). Interpretation raises further problems. Thus is rural violence to be treated as a reflection of intolerable living conditions or of envy—or is it to be considered a necessary cost of a desirable social change?

Clues on the degree of national independence include the proportion of capital inflows in exchange receipts, the proportion of the supply of capital goods (or intermediates) which is imported, the proportion of assets, especially subsoil assets, owned by foreigners, and the extent to which one trading partner dominates the patterns of aid and trade. But there are also qualitative indicators such as the existence of foreign military bases and overflying rights, and the extent to which the country follows the lead of one of the great powers in the United Nations.

THE COMPATIBILITY OF INDICATORS

This section raises the problem of weighing and comparing different indicators, a major indicator problem. It is, of course, impossible to explore all its aspects here, but it may be useful to indicate some major possibilities of inconsistency and how serious these seem to be.

On the face of it, there is a strong causal interrelation between the three leading indicators. Development on any of them implies, or helps bring about, or may even be a necessary condition for, development on one or more of the others. To reduce unemployment is to remove one of the main causes of poverty and inequality. A reduction in inequality will of course reduce poverty, *ceteris paribus*.

But are other things equal? Does lowering the concentration of income imply a slower rate of economic growth—and growth is, as we have seen, in the long run a necessary condition for eliminating poverty. And would slower growth impair employment prospects? There is a well-known, indeed classical, argument that inequality generates savings and incentives and thus promotes economic growth and employment.

I find the argument that the need for savings justifies inequality unconvincing in the Third World today. Savings propensities are after all very low precisely in countries with highly unequal distributions; the industrial countries with less concentration of income have, by contrast, much higher savings propensities. Savings are, of course, also affected by the absolute level of incomes, but the explanation of this paradox must in part lie in the high consumption standards of an unequal society.

Moreover, the rich in most countries tend to have extremely high propensities, not merely to spend, but to spend on goods and services with a high foreign exchange content, and, for countries suffering from an acute foreign exchange bottleneck, this is a major obstacle to development.[19] It is true that import demand can be held in check by administrative controls, but this leads to the elaboration of a bureaucratic apparatus which is expensive, especially in terms of valuable organizing ability, and which in some countries becomes riddled with corruption. In fact, the result of import control is often to create a protected and highly profitable local industry, which itself depends heavily on imports of intermediate products and capital goods, and remits abroad a large flow of money in profits, interest, royalties, licence fees and service charges of various sorts.[20] In any case, in a highly unequal society, personal savings often flow abroad or go into luxury housing and other investment projects of low or zero priority for development, or even for growth.

The argument that only inequality can provide the incentives that are necessary is also obviously of limited validity in a country where there are barriers of race or class or caste to advancement. Still, we cannot dismiss it out of hand. The needs for private entrepreneurial talent vary according to the circumstances of different economies, but there are very few where this need is small. Countries relying on growing exports of manufactures, as many do, depend heavily on the emergence of businessmen with the drive to penetrate foreign markets. All countries depend in some degree on the appearance of progressive farmers. Will these emerge without financial rewards on a scale that will make nonsense of an egalitarian policy? Are rising profits of companies, especially foreign companies, an inevitable feature of growth in many countries? Or are we exaggerating the importance of financial incentives? Can other non-financial rewards partially take their place?[21] Can social incentives be developed to a point where people will take on such tasks with little or no individual reward (as the governments of China and Cuba are trying to procure)?

The compatibility of growing equality and rising output and employment has recently become doubtful for an additional set of reasons. Can the people who are professionally necessary be kept in the country if they earn only a small fraction of which they could earn elsewhere? How much unemployment will their departure involve, because their labour is complementary to that of the rest of the labour force? Yet what are the costs in terms of human welfare and even efficiency if they are prevented from leaving?[22]

On the other hand, there are also very serious reasons for questioning the compatibility of *in*equality and the growth of income and employment. One is implied by the discussion of the composition of consumption above. Can a manufacturing industry be created to correspond to the structure of demand that arises in a highly inequitable society (leaving aside the question of whether it *should* be created)? Will production rise rapidly if the proportion of the labour force which is too badly nourished for full manual and mental work is only sinking slowly? Can the government obtain the co-operation of the population in wage restraint, and in many other ways that are necessary for development, if there is visible evidence of great wealth which is being transmitted from generation to generation, so that the wage earner sees his children and his children's children doomed indefinitely to subordinate positions? Or if there is little prospect of reducing unemployment? Can political leaders under such circumstances mobilize the energies of the population and break down social customs which obstruct development, especially in rural areas?

I do not pretend to know the answers to this complex of questions, which point to a set of 'internal contradictions' in the development processes more severe than those to which Marx drew attention. Any answer must in any case be specific to the country concerned. All I would say is that such questions have usually been ignored in the past, leading to a failure to appreciate the damaging consequences of inequality.

Yet another set of questions arises out of the potential inconsistency between employment in the short-run and employment in the longer term—which is often formulated as a conflict between employment and growth. There has recently been much discussion of this [*Stewart and*

Streeten, 1971]. All I would say is that here too the conflict has been ex-aggerated. It would after all be surprising if the mobilization of all the above labour in a typical economy caused anything but a big rise in output.

My original paper, to which I referred in the first footnote, went on to discuss the consistency between these economic objectives and those mentioned above, in the political and social planes—political order and liberty, independence and education. I will not go over this ground here—it would take us rather far from the subject of development indicators (the interested reader can turn to the references given in that paper—though this is not to deny that political and economic dimensions of development are connected, certain political systems are incompatible with progress towards equality, because of the relationship between the distribution of income and political power.

IMPLICATIONS FOR PLANNING

The most important use of development indicators is to provide the targets for planning. The realization that the national income is in itself an inadequate yardstick of development implies a recognition that national income targets are not very relevant. We need instead targets for poverty, employment and income distribution, specifying some of the dimensions of the structure of society at which we are aiming.

The difference in approach is more profound than it seems. Formerly the basic technique consisted in extrapolating past trends and choosing investment patterns that would produce an acceptable increase in national income in a five-year period, tacitly assuming many constraints as given—thus consumption patterns were projected in a way that assumed little or no change in income distribution or in tastes or attitudes. Now we must try to envisage what might be a satisfactory pattern at some time in the future, in terms not only of production and employment structures, but of the patterns of income distribution, consumer demand and jobs, and then work backwards, to see if there is any plausible path for getting there.

The econometrician searches for planning models with multiple objec-tives, in response to this challenge. But perhaps the task is much simpler: to lift every family above a poverty line, based on food requirements, bare minimum though it may be. To achieve this must imply the elimina-tion of poverty and unemployment and (especially if the time span is short) a reduction in inequality. It implies setting target incomes for various sizes of families and working out what measures would be needed to achieve these (the measures may include not only employment creation, but also welfare schemes such as special food programmes for children, pensions, etc.). The final step is to estimate what measures need to be taken in policy areas such as taxation and incomes.

This approach raises statistical problems. In the first place, sufficiently detailed income and expenditure studies are rarely available; even if they were, there would be problems of relating poverty lines to household composition, referred to above. Further, it would be hard to incorporate complicated indicators in development models and one might have to settle for something as crude as a minimum household income. Convert-ing targets into policies raises further problems because of the many different influences on the income of the poor and because typically there is no machinery for straightforward fiscal redistribution. But the approach is nevertheless worth pursuing—its difficulties are no excuse for persisting with inappropriate, even dangerously misleading, planning models designed to maximize economic growth.

To concentrate on the elimination of poverty implies that increased income for the rest of the population is irrelevant so long as there is undernourishment, especially of children. So be it. We must however, recognize the risk that some redistributive strategies *may* in some circumstances hamper economic growth and thus the more fundamental long-term solution of the problem of poverty.

INTERNATIONAL DEVELOPMENT

The criteria suggested above can in principle be applied to any unit—a village, a province, a nation, a continent or the world. Let me in closing refer briefly to indicators of world development. Basically the same concepts of poverty and employment apply, but in the case of inequality we are now primarily concerned with comparisons between incomes of different nations, as a guide to the policy tasks which face the rich countries if they are to contribute to the development of the poor.

There has been progress, especially since the 1930s, on the poverty criterion; the proportion of the whole human population living below any subsistence line must have fallen. But total overt world unemployment must have grown, since the emergence of unemployment in the Third World must numerically outweigh the decline of unemployment in the industrial countries. In recent years, in any case, unemployment has risen in the latter too, so there can be no doubt of the world trend (though it is not very meaningful to add together national statistics for something like unemployment which takes so many forms). Moreover, since the middle of the last century enormous gaps have opened between rich countries and poor: inequality on the present scale is an entirely new phenomenon, as papers by Simon Kuznets [*1971, pp. 27ff.; 1966, pp. 390–400*] and Surendra Patel [*1964*] have brought out.

Economic inequality between nations, like inequality within them means differences in status and power, poisoning the attitudes of men towards each other. This, again as on the national level, means growing tensions between races, broadly in this case (as also inside many countries) between the whites and the remainder. Moreover, the incompatibility of inequality with the elimination of poverty is clearer for development on the international than on the national plane. The seepage, through many channels, of the consumption habits of rich countries has contributed to unemployment in poorer countries (see above), and probably also meant slower economic growth. The transfer of technologies designed for rich countries has had similar effects; available technologies are becoming increasingly inappropriate for the worlds needs. The growing difference in *per capita* incomes also stimulates the 'brain drain' and exerts an upward pull on professional salaries in poor countries. Thus national and international inequality are linked.[23]

When we consider the world scene, it is wrong to talk about 'development', on the criteria suggested above. One cannot really say that there has been development for the world as a whole, when the benefits of technical progress have accrued to minorities which were already relatively rich. To me, this word is particularly misleading for the period since the war, especially the 'development decade' when the growth of economic inequality and unemployment may have actually accelerated. (The prospect of a 'second development decade' is daunting: a repetition of the 1960s with unemployment and inequality rising still further, would be socially, economically and politically disastrous whatever the pace of economic growth!)

The measurement of international inequality raises its own set of conceptual problems. Egalitarians like myself face a theoretical paradox. If we argue that the national income is an inappropriate measure of a nation's development, we weaken the significance of a growing *per capita* income 'gap' between rich nations and poor. However, there is really no alternative—a world income distribution by size, showing the magnitude of absolute poverty, would be immensely difficult to construct.

There are, moreover, special conceptual difficulties about international comparisons of income. Comparisons of incomes have limited significance when life styles are so different (affecting among other things the proportion of activity covered by cash transactions and thus included in 'income'), and when there are differences in climate.

A familiar measurement problem is the inapplicability of exchange rates as means of converting incomes in different currencies to a standard of comparison (such as the U.S. dollar). Attempts have been made to prepare exchange rates more appropriate for measuring the true purchasing power of different currencies, but these run up against well-known problems of weighting.[24]

Still, we must not fall into the familiar trap of criticizing statistics to the point where we deny them any meaning. Despite all its limitations (including the additional one of defining a 'rich' country) the statement that during the first 'development decade' the ratio between the average income of rich countries and poor has increased from about 12:1 to about 15:1 is not entirely lacking in content, either morally or analytically. It illustrates the widespread impact on poor countries of increasingly inappropriate salaries, consumption patterns and technologies, aggravating their own intractable problems of inequality and unemployment.

One thing this critique suggests the need for the continued worldwide development of subsidiary indicators mentioned above, such as infant mortality rates, calorie and protein consumption, and the incidence of diseases of poverty and under-nourishment.

There are of course political dimensions to international as to national development. A big step was taken in the first post-war decade with the creation of a whole system—the United Nations and its agencies. But since then progress has been very gradual, due basically to the unwillingness of the rich countries to limit their sovereignty and accept the authority of international organizations. The continued eruption of wars is an eloquent indicator of a lack of political progress which goes far to explain the negative development of the world as a whole.

NOTES

1. Thus in Trinidad the growth in *per capita* income averaged more than 5 per cent a year during the whole period 1953–68, while overt unemployment showed a steady increase to more than 10 per cent of the labour force.

2. Suppose, for example, that a perspective plan specified that *per capita* income of Brazil doubled in the next thirty years, but assumed no change in distribution or in the proportion unemployed. Then at the turn of the century, a big landowner in the Matto

Grosso could run four cars, instead of two, and a peasant in the North-East could eat two kilogrammes of meat a year instead of one. His son might well be still out of work. Could we really call that 'development'?

3. These dimensions are discussed in Mrs Baster's introduction.

4. Even for countries at a high level of development in any sense, the use of national income as an indicator is being widely challenged, e.g. by Mishan [1967], on the grounds that the environmental costs are ignored.

5. In an interesting paper Divatia and Bhatt [1969] put forward a different index of development potential, based on fundamental factor inputs such as capital and skills (though it is misleadingly described as a measure of the 'pace of development'). Movements in such an index could foreshadow what the future pace of economic growth could be. The index for India, for example, is encouraging because it shows a rate of increase twice as fast as the real national income. But, of course, it does not follow that growth potential *will* be released, let alone that development will take place.

6. This use of the national income had been developed by Colin Clark [1937]. In fact the great spurt forward in national income statistics in the 1930s and 1940s was due largely to the unemployment problem, although also to the need to quantify alternative wartime policies.

7. In addition, indirect taxes of various kinds on luxuries are relatively heavy, so such biases are particularly severe when market prices are used as weights.

8. For example, is a journey to work really an end product, as national estimators assume (especially a journey on a metropolitan underground railway!)? Additional issues are now being posed in industrial countries by the failure of national income to allow for the costs of environmental destruction, i.e. to be a sufficiently 'net' concept in that sense.

9. Every so often a researcher tries to draw conclusions about trends in *per capita* food consumption, which of course simply means revealing the implications of assumptions made by official statisticians.

10. There is an upward bias as well. The share of output covered by official statistics, and included in the national income, tends to rise, partly because a growing proportion of output passes through the hands of organized business, which is more adequately covered by official statistics, but also partly because of the general improvement in data collection.

11. The U.N. Statistical Office's 'A Complementary system of Statistics of the Distribution of Income, Expenditure and Wealth' is a useful starting-point.

12. Various poverty lines in India, where there has been much work on this question, are discussed by Fonseca [1970].

13. See papers by Abel-Smith, Bagley, Rein and Townsend in Townsend [1970].

14. This problem was first recognized by Rowntree [1901] in his classic enquiry in York, leading him to distinguish between 'primary' and 'secondary' poverty—the latter referring to the poverty of those who could afford the nutritional minimum but do not in fact attain it.

15. See, however, an interesting pair of articles by Minhas [1970] and Bardhan [1970], which show that even using the same criterion of poverty (one proposed in 1962 by a distinguished group of economists to the Planning Mission) very different conclusions can be reached on trends in the proportions lying below the poverty line through using different sources of consumption data, different allowances for price changes and different interpolation procedures.

16. Several indicators can be combined to give us an indicative profile of the prevalence of poverty in a nation, such as the U.N. Research Institute for Social Development has been experimenting with in Geneva. In fact they have taken a step further and produced a tentative 'development indicator', a weighted average of various series. The Institute's investigations of multiple associations are interesting and worth while, but we should not fall into the trap (as we could, although the Institute's Director warns us against it) of treating this indicator as 'normative'. It simply measures the extent to which a country has advanced along a path indicated by data from countries at different states of progress; see UNRISD [1969].

17. See I.L.O. [1970]. The point is made there that the measurement of unemployment depends very much on the dimension of the problem that concerns one—unemployment as a cause of personal frustration, low income or loss of output.

18. The Pareto coefficient, on the other hand, which long had its advocates, is expressly limited to measuring distribution among higher incomes.

19. To draw the conclusion that the income distributions should be changed, one

has to assume that Engel curves are non-linear, but this seems not to need specifying. Consumption of such luxuries is zero over a considerable income range.

20. See I.L.O. [*1970*] for a discussion of the compatibility of a high concentration of income with full employment. Unfortunately most theoretical texts concentrate on the relation between income distribution, savings and growth, ignoring the more important effects via the composition of consumption.

21. Though, of course, these imply inequalities of other types, even if only of social prestige.

22. I have dealt with these issues elsewhere [*Seers, 1971*].

23. See Seers [*1971*] and Jolly and Seers [*1970*].

24. Although this problem takes the form of finding the right expenditure weights for a price deflator, what we are actually doing is obtaining price weights for quantity comparisons, and this is extremely hard when price structures vary so much (see above). Analogous difficulties arise whenever comparisons are made between regions of a country (due to geographical variations in prices and consumption patterns) but much less severely.

REFERENCES

Bardhan, Pranab K., 1970, 'On the Minimum Level of Living and the Rural Poor', *Indian Economic Review*, Vol. 5, April.

Clark, Colin, 1937, *National Income and Outlay*, London: Macmillan.

Divatia, V. V., and Bhatt, V. V., 1969, 'On Measuring the Pace of Development', *Quarterly Review*, Banco Nazionale del Lavoro, No. 89, June.

Fonseca, A. J., 1970, 'The need-based Wage in India: A Computerized Estimate', reprinted from *Wage Policy and Wage Distribution in India*, Bombay: University of Bombay.

I.L.O., 1970, *Towards Full Employment*, Geneva: International Labour Office.

Jaffe, A. J., 1969, 'Notes on Family Income Distribution in Developing Countries in Relation to Population and Economic Changes'; paper given at meeting of International Association for Research in Income and Wealth, August; to be published in *Estadistica*, Inter-American Statistical Institute, No. 104.

Jolly, Richard, 1969, *Planning Education for African Development*, Nariobi: East Africa Publishing House.

Jolly, Richard, and Seers, Dudley, 1970, 'The Brain Drain and the Development Process', proceedings of the International Economic Association Conference to be published in E. A. G. Robinson (ed.), *The Gap Between the Rich and the Poor Countries*, London: Macmillan.

Kuznets, Simon, 1966, *Modern Economic Growth*, Studies in Comparative Economics No. 7, New Haven: Yale University Press.

Kuznets, Simon, 1971, *Economic Growth of Nations: Total Output and Production Structure*, Cambridge, Mass.: Belknap.

Lydall, Harold, 1968, *The Structure of Earnings*, Oxford: Clarendon Press.

Minhas, B.S., 1970, 'Rural Poverty, Land Redistribution and Development', *Indian Economic Review*, Vol. 5, April.

Mishan, E. J., 1967, *The Costs of Economic Growth*, London: Staples Press.

Patel, Surrendra, 1964, 'The Economic Distance Between Nations', *Economic Journal*, Vol. 74, March.

Rowntree, B. Seebohm, 1901, *Poverty: A Study of Town Life*, London: Macmillan.

Sametz, A. W., 1968, 'Production of Goods and Services: The Measurement of Economic Growth' in E. Sheldon and W. B. Moore (eds.), *Indicators of Social Change: Concepts and Measurements*, New York: Russell Sage Foundation.

Scrimshaw, N. S., and Gordon, J. E. (ed.), 1968, *Malnutrition, Learning and Behaviour*, Cambridge, Mass.: M.I.T. Press.

Seers, Dudley, 1971, 'The Transmission of Inequality' in Robert K. A. Gardiner (ed.), *Africa and the World*, London: Oxford University Press.

Stewart, Frances, and Streeten, Paul, 1971, 'Conflicts between Output and Employment Objectives' in Ronald Robinson and Peter Johnston (eds.), *Prospects for Employment Opportunities in the Nineteen Seventies*, London: Her Majesty's Stationery Office.

Townsend, Peter (ed.), 1970, *The Concept of Poverty*, London: Heinemann.

UNRISD, 1969, *Research Notes No. 2*, July, Geneva: United Nations Research Institute for Social Development.

Post Script

The New Meaning of Development

The republication of this article provides an opportunity for self-justification. Yet rereading the paper, I cannot avoid the impression that it was written by someone else. So of course it was. It was composed by somebody living nearly a decade ago who had only recently returned to academic life after many years spent mostly in 'operational' roles. Its author had naturally no foreknowledge of the rapidly evolving world of the 1970s, nor of the professional jobs that would modify once more his attitude to 'development'. I shall take this opportunity to draw the lessons of what has happened in the intervening years for how we should view 'development', and to suggest the practical implications.

GROWTH AND DEVELOPMENT

It seems much more than a decade since 'The Meaning of Development' was published. The common basis of development studies and policy-making was still very simple in 1969: in order to solve social problems, such as unemployment, and achieve respectable status as modern nations, poor countries needed 'development', which could be measured by GNP. In fact, economic growth *was* development: this could be accelerated with the help of trade and aid and/or private capital from countries already 'developed'. If growth was in fact not fast, the reason must lie in 'obstacles', such as economic nationalism. Questions of distribution tended to be brushed aside: 'We must bake a bigger cake before discussing how to cut it up'. Inequality was (regrettably) necessary to generate savings and provide incentives. If growth were fast enough, income could easily be redistributed later—indeed that would happen automatically.

This basically neo-classical paradigm had been already losing credibility in the 1960s. To generalize very drastically, the social problems of 'developed' countries were being rediscovered and concern was spreading about the environmental costs of economic growth. The gap between *per capita* incomes of 'developed' and 'developing' countries was apparently growing even in relative terms, despite large transfers of capital and technology.[1] Even those developing countries enjoying fast growth had not after all achieved the political status or the social equity that had been expected and hoped for. Pakistan was a conspicuous example. Income distribution apparently remained highly concentrated,[2] not merely in very poor countries, but also in those of Latin America where *per capita* income was approaching 'European' levels. Power was increasingly concentrated in the hands of those who benefited from growth, and used more and more repressively to preserve these benefits. Even open unemployment was refusing to wither away, which was politically embarrassing: so questions were being raised about the appropriateness of consumption patterns that required heavy foreign exchange expenditures and of labour-saving techniques that accompanied both aid and private investment.

25

c

Cultural lags protect paradigms long after they have lost relevance. The neo-classical growth paradigm has been remarkably tenacious—in fact, it still survives in places. It has suited so many interests. It has been highly acceptable to governments that want to slur over internal ethnic or social problems. It has offered (not only in the hands of Walt Rostow) a basis for aid policies to inhibit the spread of communism. It has provided international and national agencies with an 'objective' basis for project evaluation, and goals for what should be called the Second Growth Decade. It has generated almost endless academic research projects and stimulated theorists to construct elaborate models. It has not been fundamentally unacceptable to economistic modernisers across a broad political spectrum, including Marxists as well as members of the Chicago school. Above all, as a paradigm it is very simple.

The author of 'The Meaning of Development' could have taken the position that to use 'development' as a synonym for growth had so debased the word that it could no longer be used by honest people. But he decided, probably correctly, to propose that it should be redefined rather than abolished. 'Development' still carried much goodwill and political force; besides it had been incorporated in the titles of research institutes and international and national agencies.[7] So this article, 'The Meaning of Development', said, in a nutshell, that growth was in itself insufficient, indeed perhaps socially damaging: a country was not enjoying 'development' unless in addition inequality, unemployment and poverty were declining.

Not really very original. The paper should be seen as just one articulation in a period of drastic change in professional attitudes. If it attracted some attention, this was partly because it was presented at an SID World Congress—and one function of such gatherings is to legitimise unorthodox attitudes whose hour has arrived. It also seemed rather shocking: wasn't the over-riding importance of economic growth *obvious*?

REDISTRIBUTION AND DEVELOPMENT

But attitudes had already started to change. Work on social indicators had been gathering momentum in the 1960s. In 1970, the ILO launched the first of its series of missions under the World Employment Programme, which were basically about distribution. A number of models were subsequently devised to draw the policy implications from distributive goals, with much discussion of the trade-off between growth and distributional or employment objectives.[3] Their general theme was summed up in the title of the IBRD-IDS study 'Redistribution with Growth'.[4] The message to aid agencies was to take account of the social consequences of aid and to try to reach the poorest, especially in rural areas. For planning departments, the implication was to concentrate on the satisfaction of 'basic needs', defined in rather narrowly material terms, and for statistical offices to measure the incidence of poverty.

Yet there is already an air of unreality about this whole approach. Governments (even in countries which have received the ILO comprehensive missions—Colombia, Sri Lanka, Iran, Kenya, Philippines) have done little to change distribution.[5] The basic assumption of the development profession is that they need technical help to do so. Radical critics, on the other hand, pointing to political interest rather than technical capacity, have repeatedly posed quite a simple question in one form or another: why should those with economic and political power give it away, as these policies require, especially to the rural poor?[6] The implication drawn by some is that social progress will be indefinitely prevented by a homogeneous ruling class until it is in due course overthrown in a revolution.

That seems to require an even more simplistic political model. Still, the question about the feasibility of redistribution does lead one to the sources of power both inside and outside countries, and to not merely economic and political influences, but also cultural ones. Indeed, cultural forces obviously (*pace* Karl Marx) shape the way people perceive their material needs. Elites, in particular, including those deciding and administering policy, are clearly determined to enjoy styles of consumption far beyond the reach of the great majority of their fellow citizens; and architects and engineers almost as obstinately prescribe completely inappropriate techniques.

Actually, the author of 'The Meaning of Development' did touch on the main source of these cultural forces. Human requirements, he said (but only in a footnote), are not purely economic; 'they include . . . citizenship of a nation that is truly independent, both economically and politically'.[7] Why did he not see the link? The inertia of consumption and production patterns was obviously in part attributable to external links. True independence was not merely one of the intrinsic objectives, but also a *condition* (though insufficient in itself of course) for achieving the rest.

SELF-RELIANCE AND DEVELOPMENT

The 'oil crisis' of the 1970s really shook the conventional paradigm. It revealed starkly the cost of the continued economic and technological dependence of most countries, and underlined warnings about the limited capacity of the earth to sustain fast economic growth of the old type.

The time is indeed ripe for another critical look at the meaning of development. One could—even more easily than in 1969—defend the view that the word 'development' is too tarnished to be usable. The political and institutional reasons for retaining it still apply, however, and once more the way forward is to redefine it rather than reject it completely. The essential element to add—as is being widely recognized—is self-reliance.

We do not yet understand much about what self-reliance implies for development strategies,[8] but some of the economic aspects are obvious enough. They include reducing dependence on imported necessities, especially basic foods, petroleum and its products, capital equipment and expertise. This would involve changing consumption patterns as well as increasing the relevant productive capacity. Redistribution of income would help, but policies would also be needed to change living styles at given income levels—using taxes, price policies, advertising and perhaps rationing. In many countries, self-reliance would also involve increasing national ownership and control, especially of sub-soil assets, and improving national capacity for negotiating with transnational corporations.

There are other implications as well, especially in cultural policy. These are more country-specific, but as a general rule, let us say that 'development' now implies, *inter alia*, reducing cultural dependence on one or more of the great powers—i.e. increasing the use of national languages in schools, allotting more television time to programmes produced locally (or in neighbouring countries), raising the proportion of higher degrees obtained at home, etc.

On this approach, 'development plans' would henceforward not put the main emphasis on overall growth rates, or even on new patterns of distribution. The crucial targets would be for (i) ownership as well as output in the leading economic sectors; (ii) consumption patterns that economized on foreign exchange (including imports such as cereals and oil); (iii) institutional capacity for research and negotiation; (iv) cultural goals like those suggested above, depending on the country concerned. The Third Malaysian Plan (1976) partially reflects this approach, though it has of course been the basis of Japanese development strategy for a century.

Self-reliance has its own implications for the work of statistical offices.[9] These would need to concentrate less on 'national accounts' than on tables for key sectors and for the transnational corporations; less too on patterns of production than consumption; not so much anyway on economic, or even 'social', indicators as on technical and cultural statistics.

Of course, an emphasis on reducing dependence does not necessarily mean aiming at autarchy. How far it is desirable or even possible to go in that direction depends on a country's size, location and natural resources; on its cultural homogeneity and the depth of its traditions; on the extent to which its economy needs imported inputs to satisfy consumption patterns which have to be taken—at least in the short term—as political minima. The key to a development strategy of the type suggested is not to break all links, which would almost anywhere be socially damaging and politically unworkable, but to adopt a *selective* approach to external influences of all types.

One may well query whether this is any more feasible politically than 'redistribution with growth'. Why should the elites be any more willing to co-operate in this sort of 'development', which would also deprive them of many of the goods and services they consider essential to being part of the modern world? Basically, the answer is that such a programme may appeal to what seems in many countries to be a stronger force than social conscience—nationalism. This may be more likely to outweigh short-term material interests, as is shown by wartime experience in many countries.

Moreover, whereas redistributive policies provoke countervailing forces which often succeed in turning the clock back, moves towards self-reliance may become cumulative.[10] Increased cultural independence not merely has direct economic effects, it also strengthens the political leadership's motivation to make further reductions in dependence and weakens the internal opposition to these.

THE GEOGRAPHICAL EXTENSION OF DEVELOPMENT STUDIES

There is an additional implication, which is perhaps more important still. For if 'development' is now not primarily about *per capita* income, but also about distribution, and even more about the national capacity to negotiate with transnational corporations, and to cope with their technological innovations and their cultural impact, then it is not just needed in 'developing' countries, but in *all* countries.

This shift of emphasis is really crucial. It relieves us in 'developed' countries (following the increasingly misleading UN terminology) of paternalism. We would cease offering to solve other people's problems; instead, 'development', on this definition, involves our all working on *common* worldwide problems, while, paradoxically, keeping national interests (long-term of course) firmly in mind. The door would, moreover, be opened for the transfer of theories and experience from 'developing' to 'developed' countries, a possibility merely hinted at in 'The Meaning of Development'. This would be most obviously helpful in countries of the European periphery, such as Portugal and Greece, but also nearly as obviously in Italy and Britain, countries suffering from typical symptoms of 'underdevelopment': chronic inflation alongside chronic unemployment, and therefore resistant to Keynesian or monetarist remedies.[11]

The simple step of redefining development in this way is thus not by any means purely semantic: it changes one's whole perception of the world. For most professional purposes, to talk of the 'Third World' becomes almost meaningless, although the political alliance between OPEC members and the ex-colonies still has some vitality, so the concept has a few years of life yet.[12]

In any case, the cultural lag before this new definition is accepted is likely to be particularly long. Besides challenging a political alliance which is not ineffective, and powerful commercial interests, it threatens the comfortable academic ghetto of 'development studies' and it is also much more difficult for aid officials (and members of aid lobbies) to accept. It implies that the main way in which they could improve the world is not through increasing aid (though this is still needed in some countries), or even channelling it to people in greatest social need, but by curbing the power of the transnational corporations and limiting cultural pressures of which they themselves are a part.

I realize I am striking some notes that may seem even more shocking to some readers than 'The Meaning of Development' (and this article is not likely to be so extensively reprinted). Many, especially of the older generation, will find uncomfortable the implicit scepticism about the power of humanitarian motives and the explicit endorsement of nationalism, including our own—which ceases to be an 'obstacle' to development, and becomes instead part of the very essence of it. However, this new definition would not be at all incompatible with the praiseworthy reform of SID now in train.

September 1977   DUDLEY SEERS
                                               Institute of Development Studies

NOTES

1. However, as was suggested in 'The Meaning of Development'—perhaps not forcefully enough—economic growth cannot be measured in predominantly rural countries because of the lack of data on rural economic activities. See 'Seers versus Lipton on Urban Bias' (IDS *Discussion Paper* 116, 1977).

2. Income distributions are also (unfortunately) impossible to measure in most countries for the reasons given in the previous footnote. The evidence seems, however, overwhelming, if one also makes use of various types of data—social indicators, household budget surveys, etc.

3. Actually, since many goods and services included in the national product carry price weights which it would be difficult to defend for welfare comparisons (some goods and services are of negative social value), the policy dilemmas may not be so acute as they seem.

4. Oxford 1974. The first person to use this phrase was Hans Singer, co-leader with Richard Jolly of the ILO Mission to Kenya. The strategy proposed in this mission report was summarised as 'Redistribution from Growth'; later generalised in the IBRD/IDS study.

5. There was also a mission to Sudan, but it is too early to say yet whether its recommendations will also be shelved.

6. See, for example, 'The politics of redistribution with growth' by Colin Leys (IDS *Bulletin*, Vol. 7, No. 2, 1975) and the reply in the same issue by Richard Jolly.

7. The same footnote also referred to freedom of speech. Like political independence, this might be included as one of the 'basic needs'.

8. We could do with a study which might be called 'Greater Independence with Redistribution and Growth'. There are of course complex connections between distribution and independence (and possible trade-offs): I do not have the space to discuss these here.

9. See 'Statistical Needs for Development' (IDS *Communication* 120, 1977).

10. Unless blocked by external military intervention (a possibility always to be guarded against and requiring adequate defence expenditures to make such intervention expensive).

11. See 'North Sea Oil: The Application of Development Theories' by some of the faculty and students on the Sussex M.Phil course of 1975–77 (IDS *Communication* 121, 1977). Also, "Back to the Ivory Tower? The Professionalisation of Development Studies and their Extension to Europe" (IDS *Bulletin*, Vol 9, No 2) and *Underdeveloped Europe: Studies in Core-Periphery Relations,* ed D. Seers, M-L. Kiljunen and B. B. B. Schaffer (Harvester Press, 1978).

12. See 'A new look at the 3-world classification' (IDS *Bulletin* Vol. 7, No. 4, 1976). A revised version is due to appear as 'Patterns of Dependence' in *Transnational Capitalism and National Development; Studies in the Theory of Dependency,* ed J. Villamil (Harvester Press, 1978).

A Critique of
Development Economics in the U.S.

*E. Wayne Nafziger**

The trickle of disaffection with the orthodox literature on the economics of poor countries in the 1950s has enlarged to a deluge of discontent in the last decade. By the early 1970s, even major contributors to the field were complaining that the study of the field did not add greatly to the understanding of poverty in the underdeveloped world, nor to the bag of tools useful for policy [*Higgins, 1973: 1380; Meier, 1970: 59-60*].

Several intellectual currents have converged to produce this malaise. Even in the early years of the offerings of development economics in universities in the U.S., a few economists, especially from outside the country, argued that Anglo-American economic principles have only a limited applicability to a comprehension of the problems of economically underdeveloped countries [e.g. *Singer, 1950; Prebisch, (original 1950); Myrdal, 1957; Seers, 1963*].

Fundamental criticism of existing conceptions of reality in development studies originated in Latin America and continental Europe, and to a lesser extent in Asia and Africa, all with some 'inside' perspective on the weaknesses of dependent economies, rather than in the U.S., where national interests and wealth made available relatively greater funds and intellectual resources for the study of underdeveloped countries (see Merton [1972] on the advantages to scholarship that come from 'truths' perceived by Insiders). Some of the major themes of these dissenters have been: the disharmony of interests between economically less-developed countries (LDCs) and developed countries (DCs); a rejection of the development goals of ruling élites in both LDCs and DCs; and the

---

* Associate Professor of Economics, Kansas State University, USA. Author's thanks to Irma Adelman, Henry J. Bruton, Stephen Enke, Charles P. Kindleberger, David Lehmann, Michael Lipton, Thomas E. Weisskopf, Edwin G. Olson, John A. Delehanty and Patrick J. Gormely for helpful comments.

explanation of economic underdevelopment of a given country, not merely in terms of domestic factors, but in terms of the international economy as a system.

While I share the discontent of the dissident scholars with orthodox development economics, *my purpose here is not to construct something new, but to illuminate the flaws and cracks in the existing edifice.* This article is meant to parallel recent critiques of contributions by (primarily) U.S. scholars to the study of the sociology [*Bernstein,* 1971] and the politics [*O'Brien, 1972*] of development. To simplify what would otherwise be an unmanageable task, I pay particular attention to the views of the authors of six of the leading textbooks used in the U.S.: Everett Hagen, Benjamin Higgins, Gerald Meier, Charles Kindleberger, Henry Bruton and Theodore Morgan. These six economists enjoy a wide professional influence. (The men are to be referred to collectively as the authors or the six economists.) Views presented to beginning students in textbooks are generally representative of the orientation and direction of U.S. literature in the field as a whole.

INACCURATE OR INSUFFICIENT SOCIO-POLITICAL ANALYSIS
In much of the mainstream literature in economic development, the social and political system is taken as given or a constant. The analysis of fundamental shifts in socio-political variables and non-quantitative economic ones are frequently conveniently excluded with the phrase, *ceteris paribus.* For analytical purposes, development economists generally view the economic sphere as a closed system. The focus upon only a limited number of variables—mostly economic and measurable—facilitates the use of quantitative methods, and the search for determinants of a stable equilibrium. Only a few of the major interrelationships which affect the economic realm are analysed.

The following statement is indicative of the casual attitude towards social and institutional reality of the economic analyst viewing LDCs.

> [I]n economic exposition, . . . it usually makes little or no difference whether the comparisons [of societies] are anthropologically authentic or not. Indeed, . . . it would seem to be definitely requisite in the teaching of economics to bring out principles affecting our own institutions by means of comparisons between our own and 'simpler' societies and at the same time out of the question to make the comparison refer to any particular society or social type as reported by anthropological investigations. . . . '[A] uthentic' facts are not necessarily more useful than travelers' tales based on superficial and largely false impressions . . . or even outright fiction or poetry. [*Knight, 1941: 259–60.*]

Contemporary economists in the U.S. tend to place little more emphasis on institutional accuracy than Knight did. According to Adelman, '[o]ne mark of our professional arrogance is the implicit [view] . . . that a plausible model is obviously correct, and . . . need not be checked thoroughly against a large variety of empirical, historical, and case study evidence.' [*1974: 4*] Yet, for a science to contribute to understanding and policy, it needs a continuing challenge and examination of prevailing frames of references and conceptions of reality, and a continuing feedback between hypotheses and data.

An example of such a hypothesis, which has survived without proper feedback to the data, is the widespread assumption in the literature that '[t]he organization of much of subsistence farming is such that the produce available to the workers is divided among all the people involved, more or less irrespective of individual contributions to putput.' [*Bruton, 1965: 100*] There is no empirical evidence for this assumption. In fact, field studies by economic anthropologists contradict the premise that peasant societies are characterised by populations with roughly uniform poverty [*Hill, 1968: 239–60; Dube, 1955: 167–84*, and essays by various authors on Northeast India, Hong Kong, Guatemala, and Mauritius in *Firth & Yamey, 1964*].

Even where development economists are willing to acknowledge the importance of socio-cultural and psychological variables, they tend to accept political institutions as given [*Higgins, 1968: 373*], and frequently exclude determinants of development and stagnation of a political character. Political instability is considered a problem, but there is no effort to try to explain it, and its relationship to the international economic system and domestic class system [*Meier, 1970: 116. Cf. Nafziger & Richter, 1976.*] Higgins is representative of the development economists when he indicates that 'we shall abstract from the purely political factor in economic development, not because the political factor is unimportant but because social scientists have little to say about it.' [*1968: 227.*]

The discussion of the formulation and implementation of government development policy tends to be devoid of an examination of the disparities of economic interests among sub-groups within the population. The statement that 'past failures [in development planning] are to be found mainly in an inability or unwillingness to implement development plans' [*Meier, 1970: 744*] calls for an analysis of the extent to which it is actually in the interest of the élites to achieve stated goals which indicate a high priority upon improvement in the material well-being of the low-income classes.[1] To mention another point, scepticism and resistance by peasants and workers with regard to plans result not only from their misperceptions about the 'nature of the development process' [*Bruton, 1965: 155, 246*], but also from underlying conflicts of interest between the privileged and underprivileged.

Even the emphasis upon income distribution in the literature in the 1970s has not been accompanied by analyses of the political origins of the income inequality, the economic interests that benefit and lose from increased egalitarianism, and the sequence of political change essential to implement policies to enhance the relative position of the poorest fraction of the population. The discussion of policy by Morgan [*1975: 210–12*] and Hagen [*1975: 247–49*] focuses on measures an existing government in a capitalist or mixed capitalist society can undertake to improve the extent of income equality. Hagen foregoes an examination of the 'political difficulties' in undertaking policies to reduce inequalities, and the merits of 'a full socialisation of the means of production' in the redistribution of income. In fact, although Hagen suggests that it 'would be vapid and superficial' to confine an assessment of socialism to its impact on income equality [*ibid.*], he does not discuss the relative strengths and weaknesses of socialism and capitalism in a broader context.[2]

Perhaps in their attempt to avoid making explicit their personal value presuppositions, the six development economists, five of whom have had substantial experience as consultants to government in LDCs, accept the goals and targets selected by the political, bureaucratic, and business élites. Higgins is explicit in his view of the job of the development economist when he states that 'there are enough countries where the political power élite does want economic development to keep economists busy for some time to come'. At times it is even implicit that to enter a discussion of targets alternative to those of the 'policymakers', i.e. those favoured by less influential segments of the population, is to enter the domain of normative economics, which is to be eschewed [*Higgins, 1968: 227, 373, 376–77; Bruton, 1965: 362*].

AN ETHNOCENTRIC APPROACH TO U.S. INTERNATIONAL INVOLVEMENT

The economists surveyed tend to appraise the LDCs from the perspective of U.S. standards, achievements, interests, and sympathies. There is a lack of sensitivity to explanations of the alien economy, polity, and culture in terms of its own goals, institutions, values, and character. Often the authors view underdeveloped countries through the lens of U.S. international political involvement and economic interests.[3] 'Stability in underdeveloped areas' is identified with the hegemony of the U.S. and its capitalist allies [*Higgins, 1968: 198*]. A frequent point of departure for viewing LDCs is as potential recipients of foreign aid, whose main objective, in the case of the U.S., as with 'other tools of foreign policy, is to produce the kind of political and economic environment in the world in which the United States can best pursue its own social goals.' [*Chenery, 1964: 81*]. Higgins defines 'underdeveloped [countries] in a policy sense; that is, countries "with announced goals and policies with regard to economic development and which are regarded as candidates for technical and capital assistance under the foreign aid programs of the United States and other advanced Western countries." ' [*1968: 147.*] Even Kindleberger, among the most sympathetic and least patronising of the authors, is inclined toward a viewpoint that legitimises intervention by rich and powerful donors into the internal political and economic affairs of LDCs. He argues that the position that

> [foreign] assistance should be given with no strings attached . . . is too simple and idealistic by half. Sovereignty is not inviolable, nor are internal politics sacrosanct where they stand in the way of development .. . . If the sole condition of foreign aid is that it be used effectively, the abridgment of sovereignty which comes from consultation with foreign missions, with the International Bank, or a United Nations agency is supportable. If such outside forces are to be effective, moreover, they must take positions on issues which are subjects of internal struggles, and thereby find themselves interfering in internal politics. [*1965: 374–375.*]

INSUFFICIENT CONSIDERATION OF DOMINATION AND SUBORDINATION WITHIN
THE INTERNATIONAL ECONOMIC SYSTEM

The conceptual matrix of orthodox development economics in the U.S. is
limited in its ability to explain poverty and underdevelopment. In orthodox
economics, underdevelopment is explained primarily in terms of economic
factors within a given nation-state, with little reference to the effects of the
international economy as a system. The authors regard the development of
the DCs and the underdevelopment of the LDCs as essentially unrelated
phenomena. National aspirations for rapid economic growth in the poor
countries are in the interest of, and are encouraged by, the DCs [*Meier
and Baldwin, 1957: 13*].

Except for Higgins [*1968: 161–87, 267–95, 683–93, 800–06*], the
economic impact of colonialism and post-colonial imperialism on the
DCs and LDCs is not considered [e.g. *Hagen, 1975: 73–100*.] The evidence
of economic history, including that of the period of Western colonialism,
is overlooked, with the argument that 'bygones are bygones' —that the
present situation determines the future, irrespective of how the present
arose historically from the past. In the words of one author: 'It is unnecessary to account for a situation presented to the initial conditions by
history.' [*Bruton, 1965: 90*. See also *Morgan, 1975: 143*.]

Because of the lack of consideration of the history of imperialism, a
part of the explanation for development in the West, and underdevelopment
in most of the non-Western world, is disregarded. The textbooks virtually
omit reference to the economic and geographical expansion of Europe
at the expense of non-European peoples, especially after the fifteenth
century. Empire—both formal and informal—may have facilitated the
economic development of the West through the control and stabilisation
of markets and raw material production needed for industrial growth,
and the provision of added profitable outlets for the investment of capital.
At no point is there a systematic attempt by the authors to discuss or
refute the argument that Western economic development benefited at the
expense of the non-Western world.[4] A comprehensive textbook would
be expected to at least mention the argument.

On the other side of the coin, the adverse effect of colonialism and
informal empire on presently LDCs is largely overlooked. For Meier, it
is not 'the intentional or unintentional exploitation of colonialism or
neo-colonialism which can have detrimental effects on development
efforts.' [*1970: 117*.] There is little consideration of what might have
happened if countries under formal colonial rule or informal political
suzerainty of the metropolitan powers had instead been free to direct the
development of their economies themselves—by borrowing from western
civilisation and economies as a separate autonomous system rather than
as peripheral areas integrated into the international capitalist system. To
discuss this, it is essential to analyse something absent in five of the books
—the culture and economy of the LDCs before European domination
and colonialism, and the impact of formal and informal empire, and post-
colonial dependency. The common historical experience of virtually all
LDCs includes the past economic and political domination under
colonialism or informal empire by the now DCs. The crucial relation-

ships of the now DCs with present LDCs have disrupted the pre-existing fabric of these societies, many of which were sophisticated, cultured and wealthy before European penetration.

There may be a few instances (such as Malaya and the Gold Coast, which both had spare land) where economies responded positively, with widespread benefits, to the impact of overseas capitalism; but these are exceptions. On the other hand, India experienced economic stagnation under British colonial rule, with a decrease in the output of industrial goods (particularly handicraft articles) *per capita* from 1757 to 1857, a decline in the export of cotton manufactures in the early nineteenth century and again at the turn of the twentieth century as a result of foreign competition, and a drop in agricultural (especially food) output *per capita* from 1893–6 to 1936–46. Indonesia, a prosperous region at the beginning of the sixteenth century, suffered a marked decline in *per capita* material well-being during the period of Dutch suzerainty. In coastal West Africa, the slave trade of the sixteenth through eighteenth centuries brought about the disintegration of central authority, and colonisation primarily in the nineteenth and twentieth centuries destroyed pre-colonial trade and organised commerce in the direction required by the externally-oriented nature of the economy. Within a generation after Spanish penetration of the West Indies, the indigenous economy was ruined, and the native population virtually disappeared [*Frank, 1969: 41–2; Maddison, 1971: 53–63; Thorner and Thorner, 1962: 70–112; Griffin, 1969: 38–45; Amin, 1972.*]

Development economists single out Japan as 'the only country in recent decades to have "graduated" from the ranks of . . . an under-developed country' to an advanced country [Higgins, 1968: 617]. This dramatic progress has been attributed to adaptation of labour relationships to the 'imperatives of Japanese personality', to 'reactive nationalism', to land reform, to other instutional reform, to government assistance to private enterprise, to drastic monetary and fiscal measures, to the 'efforts of government to transfer and develop a technology suitable to Japanese conditions', and to an open economy [*ibid.: 617–9, and Hagen, 1975: 297–8*]. It is rarely indicated that these measures and adaptations would probably not have occurred had the Japanese been under Western economic domination. Conceivably, similar strategies might have been used by other Afro-Asian and Latin American countries to try to develop rapidly had they been free to borrow, adapt, innovate, and plan in light of indigenous goals and strengths.

In the subsequent part of this section, I consider the orthodox view of the benefits that LDCs received from foreign trade and investment. One model recommended for emulation by LDCs is that of Britain in the eighteenth and nineteenth centuries, at which time international trade was 'a leading sector' which served as an engine of growth [*Kindleberger, 1965: 304*]. The relevance of the British experience breaks down, however, when one recalls that international trade and output expanded rapidly during a period of the acquisition of informal and formal empire, accompanied by British military strength, political domination, and market power. Within the context of this economic and political dominance and suzerainty—which includes British control of imperial tax and tariff policy, preferential treatment of British entrepreneurs in Britain or the colonies, and the promotion of the production of inputs needed for British industry—an 'international division of labour' based upon a 'comparative advantage in real costs' was established.

Meier raises the question: 'why has not a process of export-induced development followed upon an expansion of the export sector' in LDCs? He rejects the view that integration in the international trading network might have been responsible for inhibiting development and increasing international inequality. 'A more convincing explanation [for the lack of an export-induced development] focuses on the differential effects of the various export goods [on forward and backward linkages, and the structure of demand] . . . and on market imperfections and socio-cultural impediments within a poor country.' Meier argues that foregoing the employment of surplus resources in the foreign export-oriented sector would have meant that these resources would have been idle, with no mention of the possibility of locally-based development, with part of the capital and technology acquired from DCs [*Meier, 1970: 509–13*].[5]

Foreign investment is considered mutually advantageous to the DCs and LDCs, usually without investigating the evidence on the other side. To Meier, a 'central problem . . . is for the recipient country to devise policies that will succeed in . . . encouraging a greater inflow of private foreign capital.' The major factors accounting for the sub-optimal flow of private capital to LDCs are '[c]ontrols exercised by the host country over the conditions of entry of foreign capital, regulations of the operation of foreign capital, . . . restrictions on the remittance of profits and the re-patriation of capital, . . . [and] limitations on the extent of foreign partici-pation in ownership or management.' Meier finds it important to raise the profit expectations of the prospective foreign investor, in part through the provision of public expenditures in 'developing the country's infra-structure and in ensuring a supply of trained labor.' [*1970: 297–9, 305.*] Despite the vast literature indicating that foreign firms are not significantly influenced by tax incentives [*Gordon & Grommers, 1962: Mikesell, 1962*], Higgins stresses the importance of LDCs overcoming their '[r]eluctance to make conditions attractive to foreign firms'—to offer tax schemes and incentives, and to allow foreign firms to bring their own managers and technicians [*Higgins, 1968: 567–71*].

The authors recommend an improvement in the 'investment climate' in LDCs through the liberalisation of the terms for foreign capital [e.g. *Meier, 1970: 296–8*]. Yet they do not consider the possible distortion in the post-independence structure of the ownership of industrial assets in LDCs, that ensues from foreign investment which entered in the colonial period, largely as a result of policies and rules of the game which discrimi-nated in favour of firms from the DCs. Moreover, as a result of pressures and sanctions from the DCs in the post-colonial period, existing legal commitments and regulations that permitted foreign capital and entre-preneurship to enter the country relatively freely could not be easily rescinded. Finally, the authors overlook the fact that investing countries have so often had to use threats of economic retaliation and politico-military force in order to compel LDCs to keep their economies open to foreign capital [*see Griffin, 1972: 120*].

There are a number of arguments overlooked by the authors. In general terms, the structure and growth of an LDC open to foreign investment (together with foreign trade and assistance) becomes dependent upon the nature of the development and expansion of the developed capitalist economies [*Frank, 1969: 3–17; Dos Santos, 1970*]. Let us mention some more specific arguments. The foregoing of the limited gains by foreign investment may be outweighed by increases in returns to the domestic competitors of foreign investors [*MacDougall, 1960: 13–35*]. Local resources used in the foreign sector have some opportunity cost, and contribute to a 'backwash' effect. The subordination of the acquisition of finance, technology, and high-level manpower by an LDC to developments and interests in a metropolitan economy may hamper indigenous efforts to establish a capital market, to generate appropriate technology, to acquire industrial and business experience, to develop a local bourgeoisie, and to train and educate skilled industrial manpower. Finally, as the next paragraph maintains, a major argument for overseas investment, which centres around the necessity to transfer the knowledge, skills and techniques of modern production, is of limited validity in most LDCs.

Hagen [*1975: 101–29*] and Higgins [*1968: 203*] point out the rarity of technological innovation in the LDCs, and the lack of technology available to fit their factor proportions and cultural patterns. But, under colonial rule, LDCs did not have the control to experiment and develop innovations, or to instigate institutions oriented toward innovations, needed to produce or adapt technology appropriate to their economies and cultures. In the post-independence world, LDCs are virtually entirely dependent upon the advanced capitalist countries, where the control of technology is concentrated. Müller's data on patents granted by a group of mixed and capitalist LDCs suggest that if the number of patents is weighted by their economic or technological worth (i.e. volume of sales or value added), most LDCs would find that the share of patents thus weighted, granted to foreigners, would be over 99 per cent [*1973: 126–7*]. Furthermore, international markets are organised and incentives are structured in such a way that it is usually not in the interest of a foreign enterprise to impart to indigenous counterparts the knowledge and skills upon which commercial success is based [*Weisskopf, 1972: 48*]. Multinational corporations restrict the use of technology and output in LDCs—by e.g. banning exports, limiting technology to the period of agreement, preventing modification of a technology, and requiring purchase of intermediate inputs into the technology from the country of the foreign company [*Curry, 1973*].

The tacit premise of those who neglect the history of past economic subordination seems to be that an understanding of this history has no relevance for current policy [*Bruton, 1965: 90*]. But, as suggested above, the nature of the legacy of economic dependence has important implications for present policy with regard to foreign trade, investment, technological transfer and political relations, which form a part of a total policy nexus which impinges on the domestic economy and polity.

THE CONCEPT OF 'TRADITIONAL' SOCIETY AND ECONOMY

The neglect by the six economists of the history of the LDCs, including colonialism and post-colonial dependency, is in accord with the assumption that the present LDCs resemble earlier stages in the history of the now DCs. Past economies—'primitive', ancient and medieval, and present DCs a century or two ago—are placed with present LDCs in a single category, a 'traditional economy', in contrast to the 'modern economy' of contemporary DCs. Higgins indicates that '[i]t is hard to see how one could identify a traditional society in terms other than its level of economic development.' [*1968: 175*. Also *Rostow, 1971: 4–6*.]

It is a distortion to classify today's LDCs together with the preindustrial societies of the West under the rubric 'traditional society', which implies that its underlying socio-economic features have been shaped by endogenous forces. Presumably, we need a systematic historical explanation to ascertain to what extent the socio-economic traits we observe are traditional and originate internally, and to what extent they are a product of non-traditional and exogenous forces. It could be argued that very few of the present LDCs can be considered traditional, since their societies and economies were disrupted by colonialism (or some other dependent economic and political relationship to the developed world). Many of the characteristics of what development economists have thought to be a 'traditional society' could well be an outgrowth of the last two centuries or so, when the entire fabric of the polity, society and economy of the LDCs was affected by the intrusion of the metropolitan capitalist countries. The replacement of indigenous enterprises with technologically more advanced global subsidiary companies, the formation of an unskilled labour force to work in the factories, mines and plantations, the attraction of highly educated youths to junior posts in the colonial administration service, the migration of workers from the villages to the foreign-dominated urban economic complexes, and the opening of the economy to trade with and investment from the DCs are not concomitant with the process of economic modernisation, as orthodox economists assume. Instead, the same phenomena, manifestations of the penetration of modern capitalism into archaic economic structures in the periphery, are on this interpretation the basis for the creation of underdevelopment.

The identification of societies as traditional rather than those disrupted by imperialism distorts the analysis of the determinants and concomitants of underdevelopment. For Hagen, '[t]raditional societies tend to be hierarchical and more or less authoritarian in political structure. Such structure persisted for centuries and in some societies for several millenia, up to modern times.' [*1975: 81*. Also *Morgan 1975: 37*]. Doubtless, in some cases. But it is essential to try to ascertain to what extent the hierarchy was a function of 'traditional' culture, on the one hand, or a culture shaped by an era of politico-economic subservience, on the other. In some instances, e.g. Northern Nigeria and parts of the Indian sub-continent, colonial support for a compliant indigenous political élite, who held office as long as it was advantageous to the colonial rulers, eliminated important sources of both external and internal opposition, strengthened the hands of the native élite in dealing with dissidents, and hampered indigenous political development. The role of native chiefs in Nigeria and South Asia inhibited the development of nationalism and a strong local bourgeoisie, and strengthened the concentration of land holdings among overlords and *zamindars*. In the post-colonial era, metropolitan nations, with their means of coercion (military, economic, and political power) and superior resources (resulting in aid, investment, and a dominant trade position), are able to structure their relationships with LDCs so that, even though there is a conflict of interest between the rich and poor nations in general, there is a harmony of interest between the élites of these nations. The DC develops a bridgehead in the LDC, which enables the former to maintain political and economic hegemony in the latter, and in the process support and assist those in the poor country willing to cooperate, i.e. those whose interests are in harmony with that of the rich country.

Of course, the élite of a country can be authoritarian and lack an orientation toward the economic development of the masses, even where the country has never encountered alien colonial and imperial hegemony. But for countries which have experienced foreign economic and political domination, class hierarchy, élite structure and the formation of ruling ideologies and values cannot be analysed apart from an historical examination of transnational interrelationships. A 'politically powerful group which has a big stake in maintaining the *status quo*' [*Higgins, 1968: 195*] does not spring from Jove's brow and may have even been created and strengthened during the process of colonialism or post-colonial imperialism. The present élite may be 'traditionalistic rather than choice-making' and not imbued with the 'idea of progress' [*Bruton, 1965: 113*] as a result of a social structure created in part by colonialism, and supported by neo-imperialism. Even the Indian caste system [*ibid.: 111 and Morgan, 1975: 39*], though it existed in ancient times, was strengthened by British policy in the colonial period. Hagen finds that 'the sign of éliteness in a traditional society is that the individual does not demean himself by concerning himself with the details of manual labor.' [*1975: 132*. Also *pp. 115–16, 270–1, 278*, and *Myrdal, 1968: II, 1057–61, 1369*.] The explanation may lie not only in the traditional society itself, but also in its disruption by outside conquest or domination.[6]

Those for whom today's 'modernised' societies present an image of the future of 'traditional societies' envision a movement in history from a 'rigid' social structure and underdeveloped economy to a fluid social structure and developed economy, whose archetype is the U.S. and western Europe. Comparative evidence, however, indicates that the fluidity of the prototypical modern country, the U.S., does not vary much from that of India [*Nafziger, 1975: 144–6*], with a 'caste system . . . of the ironclad variety'. [*Bruton, 1965: 111*.]

AN INADEQUATE PERSPECTIVE ON MARXISM

Where alternative approaches such as Marxism are considered, the economists use only orthodox standards of theoretical excellence in the selection of what is relevant and in the criticism of the validity of alternative theories. Higgins does not evaluate and criticise the Marxist model in terms of its own paradigm or even some 'neutral' paradigm. Rather, the model is forced into a series of equations in a neo-classical general equilibrium model, which not surprisingly, reduces the Marxian contribution to triviality. The reader is told, for example, that the three major differences between the Schumpeterian system, on the one hand, in comparison to the classical and Marxist system, are 'the introduction of the interest rate as a determinant of savings, . . . the separation of autonomous from induced investment and the isolation of "innovations" as the factor influencing autonomous investment, . . . [and] the emphasis on entrepreneurship as the vital force in the whole economy.' The interest is not 'to evaluate the Marxist system as a whole' but to 'isolate the key propositions of its pure theory of economic development.' Pure theory is conceived in terms of neo-classical analysis, with a predisposition toward capitalism and the free market, a selection of only certain relevant variables, and a neglect of the variables of class, historical and dialectical theory, and the relationship between social relations and the means of production. Marx's system thus viewed is said not to be as applicable to LDCs as Malthus' theory is [*Higgins, 1968: 76–87, 100–1*].

Higgins gives a general synthesis of Marx, Schumpeter, Harrod, Domar and Hansen which includes the fact that 'the key figure in the process of technological advance is the entrepreneur.' The basic equation, seen as a synthesis of these general theories, becomes a basis for indicating that an effective plan must encourage a higher level of private investment with the existing rate of resource discovery and technological progress, must encourage a 'long view' through promotion of confidence, and must improve the climate for foreign investment [*Higgins, 1968: 150, 156*].

Meier, in accepting Rostow's stage theory as an answer to Marx, remarks that Rostow, unlike Marx, does not 'reduce the complexities of man to a single economic dimension.' Rostow also is said to have a 'broader view of human motivation' in contrast to Marx's 'narrow view that political behavior is dependent on economic advantage.' [*1970: 92–4*.] However, Marx's explanation of the interrelationships between relations of production and the social, cultural, legal, and institutional structure of society provides the basis for a far broader view of human motivation and behaviour than that indicated by Meier.

> In the social production of their means of existance men enter into definite, necessary relations which are independent of their will, productive relationships which correspond to a definite stage of development of their material productive forces. The aggregate of these productive relationships constitutes the economic structure of society, the real basis on which a juridicial and political superstructure arises, and to which definite forms of social consciousness correspond. The mode of production of the material means of existence conditions the whole process of social, political and intellectual life. It is not the consciousness of men that determines their existence, but, on the contrary, it is their social existence that determines their consciousness. [Marx, 1904: 11.]

Furthermore, Meier asserts that Rostow's analysis 'draws upon a far wider range of historical knowledge, and is thereby more comprehensive and less doctrinaire.' [*1970: 93*]. All this is asserted, with no reference at all to Marx's work, or any attempt to even sketch a part of his theory of economic development and capitalist crisis.

It is perhaps ironic that Hagen, who recognises the key role of powerful vested interests in opposing measures that are 'economically desirable' [*1975: e.g. 357, 434*], and whose own theory attributes economic stagnation and lack of innovation to the hierarchical and authoritarian social system of traditional societies [*1962*], is so harsh in his attack on a theory which examines hierarchy, interest groups, and administrative weaknesses in a Marxian framework. According to Hagen, the major ingredients of the theory of Paul Baran, probably the foremost U.S. Marxist in the last 25 years, are '[a] special version of all of the hypotheses of peculiar barriers' of Nurkse, Singer, and Rosenstein-Rodan, and '[a] political theory [concerning an] alliance between feudal landlords, industrial royalists, and the rising bourgeois capitalist middle classes.' [*1975: 175–6.*] Since Hagen's characterisation of the thesis of Baran is devoid of a mention of class interests and conflict, historical dialectics, and the theory of comprador governments, his contribution is reduced to that comprehensible in the standard non-Marxist paradigm. Hagen has the following to say in his appraisal of Baran's analysis.

> No technical or entrepreneurial problems exist. If the ruling alliance had the will, economic development (and social progress) could proceed without difficulty.
>
> Beneath the polemics, [Baran's] thesis has a good deal in common with some of the argument presented [in Hagen's book, viz.] that the market opportunity is not seized because innovation is difficult, . . . [that] the difficulties are not surmounted . . . because insufficient innovative entrepreneurship exists, . . . [and] that the landed elites of low-income societies do not save and invest productively because their attitudes toward life constrain them. Baran agrees concerning the overt behaviour but he will have none of this coddling concerning its causes. The reason men who might act do not, he states, is that they are evil men. But this [Baran's view] of course is characterization, not analysis.
>
> If one regards the propensity of men not to save as evil, one must still ask, if one wishes to gain more than a superficial understanding, why men are evil. . . . His [Baran's] thesis will be unsatisfying except to persons who believe that the devil theory of history is adequate analysis. [*1975: 176.*]

From the Marxian point of view, these 'attitudes' toward life are not themselves primary variables, but are determined by the social relations of production corresponding to a definite stage of development of the material powers of production. For example, the attitudes and values of diligence, thrift, and punctuality may be especially emphasised during the early period of industrial capitalism.

To Baran, those concerned about the problems of a lack of supply of entrepreneurs have misplaced their emphasis. The entrepreneur is not the major figure accounting for capitalist development, but is, along with the capitalist, a figure that has benefited significantly from the age of modern capitalism. Furthermore, Baran charges that the study of entrepreneurship is ideologically oriented. Much of the literature on entrepreneurship, he contends, extols the 'genius' of the entrepreneur in the capitalist system, without trying to explain why his 'genius' turned to the accumulation of capital. In addition, the problem of entrepreneurial ability in LDCs is not its inadequacy but the composition of entrepreneurship between the various sectors of the economy [*1957: 234–7*].[7]

Contrary to Hagen, Baran neither attributes a lack of economic development to the actions of 'evil men', nor does he lack an explanation for these actions. Instead

> It is fundamental to [Baran's] Marxian approach to the study of man that there is no such thing as an external invariant, 'human nature' . . . [T]he character of man is the product of the social order in which he is born. . . '[S]ocial order' . . . encompasses the attained stage of the development of productive forces, the mode and relations of production, the form of social domination prevailing at any given time, all together constituting the *basic* structure of existing social organization. [Author's italics. *Baran, 1969*: 97–8, reprinted from the *Monthly Review, October 1959*. Compare *Morgan, 1975: e.g. p. 357*, who states that 'Businessmen are by nature individualists.'][8]

A ruling coalition whose interests are in conflict with those of the masses may, according to Baran, be exploitative and oppressive. But Baran's explanation of the contribution of the upper classes to the underdevelopment of LDCs, as indicated in the following paragraph, is far removed from a 'devil theory of history'.

Furthermore, it is unfair for Hagen to imply that Baran lacks an analysis of the role of the capitalist (entrepreneurial) and landed classes in the inhibition to capital accumulation and economic growth. To Baran, the chance for an indigenously-derived capitalist revolution in LDCs was retarded as a result of Western economic and political suzerainty, especially in the colonial period. Capitalism entered not through the growth of small competitive firms, but rather through the transfer from abroad of advanced monopolistic business. The comprador bourgeoisie, which lacked the strength to spearhead the thoroughgoing institutional change needed for major capital accumulation, was compelled to seek allies among other classes. In certain instances, the bourgeoisie tried to ally with moderate leaders of the workers and peasants to form a progressive coalition with a 'New Deal' orientation (such as the Congress Party governments under Nehru in India). For the popular movement was at the outset essentially democratic, anti-feudal, and anti-imperialist, and in support of domestic capitalism. However, the native capitalist middle-classes were either unwilling or unable to provide the leadership for a sustained economic development which would also ameliorate the poverty and subjugation of the masses. In time, the local bourgeoisie, frightened by the threat of labour radicalism and populist upheaval and their possible implications for the expropriation of capital and abolition of property ownership, were impelled into an alliance with the landed interests, and those governments supporting the foreign bourgeoisie which could provide the economic and military assistance to stave off impending disaster. The differences within this 'counter-revolutionary' coalition were not to be compared to the over-riding common interest in preventing socialism. The coalition is not capable of implementing the means needed to raise the rate of capital accumulation significantly— measures such as the adoption of a progressive tax system to eliminate non-essential consumption, the channeling of savings from the landed aristocracy into productive investment, and the undertaking of substantial public investment in sectors where private capital does not venture, where monopolistic controls block expansion, or where social overhead projects are necessary. This conservative alliance thrusts the popular forces even further along the road of radicalism and revolt, leading to further polarisa- tion. The only way out of the impasse may be revolution by workers and peasants, the expropriation of land and capital, and the establishment of a new regime based on the 'ethos of collective effort' [*Baran, 1957*].

Morgan criticises Baran for neglecting the possibility that the aims of the ruling group toward power and status could express themselves in a concern for 'the general public good. . . Some national leaders clearly have a . . . sense of values . . . [where] the general public good has been the primary goal.' [1975: 100.] Even if this is the case, the Marxist con- ceptual scheme, with its emphasis upon the economic superstructure as the great moving power of all historic events, and class interest as a basic determinant of behaviour and attitudes, would provide a framework for explaining the origin of these values.[9]

CONCLUDING REMARKS

Orthodox development economics in the U.S. has developed largely in isolation from the views of Marxism and other heterodox systems of thought. As a result, the treatment of radical economics by mainstream scholars has been inaccurate and inadequate. Furthermore, orthodox economics has been impoverished by the lack of intellectual ferment that ensues from dialogue and controversy with other approaches and paradigms. The insufficient cross-fertilisation of orthodox thought by these other views has contributed to the abstraction from politics, the lack of institutional accuracy, the ethnocentric view of international economic and political relations, the relative disregard of imperialism and neo- colonialism, the neglect of economic history, the distorted concept of the 'traditional' economy, and the inaccurate perspective on Marxism charac- teristic of U.S. development economics.

These flaws in the orthodox conception of political economy may be responsible for much of the difficulty that U.S. economists have encoun- tered in trying to adapt successfully to work in the LDCs. The following observation regarding U.S. (and Western) economics graduates working in LDCs is still substantially valid.

> There is so much for economics graduates to unlearn—and unfortunately
> the abler the student has been in absorbing the current doctrine, the more
> difficult the process of adaptation. [*Seers, 1963.*]

In order to enhance their comprehension of poverty and under- development in LDCs, American economists will need to expand their intellectual horizons beyond their limited universe of discourse to become conversant with the contributors of heterodox views in the U.S. and the rest of the world. For a major task for development economists is to devise critical tests—capable of being refuted or falsified—to determine the validity and the range of applicability of some of the hypotheses of orthodox and radical economics mentioned and implied above. But, if the thrust of this article is correct, those engaged in this task will need a background in and an understanding of Marxian economics, as well as standard economic thought.

How likely is it that development economics in the U.S. will begin to utilise insights from the radical perspective? Already there is evidence that a growing number of U.S. economists are willing to tolerate and, in some instances, encourage the development of radical political economics. An analysis of the dialectics of, for example, a deceleration in the growth of U.S. universities and foundations, a decrease in the relative remuneration of university (economics) professors, the attainment of greater political and economic self-determination by LDCs, the decline of U.S. hegemony abroad, and the development of U.S. capitalism; and the impact of these changes upon the *Weltanschauung* and intellectual perspectives of sub-communities of U.S. economists and academicians, are beyond the scope of this paper. Whatever the trend may be, it is certain to have a major effect upon the textbooks and other general works that beginning students in development economics will read.

NOTES

1. Nafziger and Richter have discussed reasons for the rejection of the development values and plans of the politico-economic élite and their foreign consultants [*1976: 100–102*].

2. Neither do any of the other five economists. See, however, an article by H. G. Johnson [in *Meier 1970: 681–7*]. In the previous edition of the book, Hagen indicates that 'It is probably a justifiable generalization that over the long run . . . private management in almost all countries tends to be more consistently efficient. . . . The rage of humiliation . . ., not economic logic, is the main cause of the socialization of industrial enterprise, and indeed of the establishment of socialist societies.' [*1968: 410*]. However, no empirical data are cited to indicate the superiority of the emphasis upon private enterprise. In fact, comparative international figures on growth in *per capita* income, which are implied in a table he presents but does not discuss, indicate a more rapid rate of growth in socialist LDCs than capitalist LDCs [*Hagen, 1968: 36–8*], although the presence of substantial margins of error in cross-cultural income comparisons are well-known.

3. Enke, an author of a textbook in development economics [*1963: vii–viii*], is especially explicit in indicating that his interest in economic development is motivated by ideological concerns arising from the gains of the Soviet Union and China in the LDCs during the Cold War.

4. Higgins' discussion of secular stagnation illustrates the blind spot of orthodox economics to the possibility that underdevelopment in the LDCs might be related to the international economic extension of the DCs. Although the tendency toward stagnation in advanced capitalist economies impels their expansion of international trade and investment, this expansion is considered 'irrelevant to the present underdeveloped countries.' [*Higgins, 1968: 152–3*.]

5. In LDCs, the problems of insufficient diversification of export production, [*Higgins, 1968: 284–6*] and the lack of 'flexibility and adaptability to move . . . resources in response to changing profit opportunities' [*Bruton, 1965: 346*] may result in balance-of-payments instability and declining terms of trade. But the authors fail to point out that these problems can frequently be attributed in part to a legacy from policies originating in the colonial period.

6. Furthermore, attitudes toward manual work are also a function of its remuneration relative to that of intellect work. This relative wage structure is itself a product of

past values, institutions and history, which, in the case of much of the non-Western world, includes the history of colonialism.

7. Much of the discussion of entrepreneurship [*Bruton, 1965: 94, 97, 254–9; Hagen, 1975: 268–299; Meier, 1970: 588; Higgins, 1968: 105, 150*], if not apologetics for ruthless capitalist exploitation, as Baran suggests [*1957: 234–7*], is a celebration of the virtues of the capitalist entrepreneur in economic growth, without a critical look at his class origins and monopoly advantage, or the impact of colonial policies on entrepreneurial supply. For an analysis of the ethnocentric view of U.S. development economists on entrepreneurship, see Nafziger [*1975*].

8. According to Morgan [*1975: 100*], Baran does not consider the necessity of relying upon 'the strongest motive (the advantage of individuals and their families)' in order to build effective incentives into any successor system to capitalism. However, Baran, like Marx, does not regard 'human nature' as invariant, but expects the selfishness and greed associated with the profit motive to decline with a shift in the ownership and control of the means of production from capitalists to workers. Moreover, implicit in Baran's discussion is the Maoist view that human beings can be socialised, educated, and indoctrinated to place more reliance on 'moral incentives' instead of 'material incentives' [*Baran, 1969: 92–111*].

9. To Morgan, governing élites utilise and adjust to a pre-existing ideology, the origin of which is not explained. E.g. '[governing groups] are impelled . . . to cater to local religions, customs, and patterns of value. They are likely, specifically, to support local economic orthodoxy, whatever it is—private enterprise, socialist, communist, co-operative; or state-directed isolationist.' [*1975: 343.*] To the Marxist, on the other hand, the existence of an ideology is a product of the material conditions in society, and the class struggle. The effort of a ruling élite to justify and legitimise their position is especially important in the creation of an ideology.

REFERENCES

Adelman, I., 1974, 'On the State of Development Economics', *Journal of Development Economics*, Vol. 1, No. 1.
Amin, S., 1972, 'Underdevelopment and Dependence in Black Africa', *Journal of Peace Research*, No. 2.
Baran, P. A., 1957, *The Political Economy of Growth*, New York: Monthly Review, Press.
Baran, P. A., 1969, *The Longer View—Essays Toward a Critique of Political Economy*, New York: Monthly Review Press.
Bernstein, H., 1971, 'Modernization Theory and the Sociological Study of Development', *Journal of Development Studies*, Vol. 7, No. 2.
Bruton, H. J., 1965, *Principles of Development Economics*, Englewood Cliffs: Prentice-Hall, Inc.
Chenery, H. B., 1964, 'Objectives and Criteria of Foreign Assistance' in G. Ranis, ed., *The United States and the Developing Economies*, New York: W. W. Norton, Co.
Curry, R. L., 1973, 'Technology Transfer to Africa: The Role of Multinational Corporations', Paper presented to the African Studies Association, November.
Dos Santos, T., 1970, 'The Structure of Dependence', *American Economic Review*, Vol. 60, No. 2.
Dube, S. C., 1955, *Indian Village*, London: Routledge and Kegan Paul.
Enke, S., 1963, *Economics for Development*, Englewood Cliffs: Prentice-Hall, Inc.
Erasmus, C. J., 1954, 'An Anthropologist Views Technical Assistance', *The Scientific Monthly*, Vol. 78, No. 3.
Firth, R. and B. S., Yamey, ed., 1964, *Capital, Saving and Credit in Peasant Societies*, Chicago: Aldine Publishing Co.
Frank, A. G., 1969, *Latin America: Underdevelopment or Revolution—Essays on The Development of Underdevelopment and the Immediate Enemy*, New York: Monthly Review Press.
Gordon, L. and Grommers, E., 1962, *United States Manufacturing Investment in Brazil*, Boston: Harvard Business School.
Griffin, K. B., 1969, *Underdevelopment in Spanish America—An Interpretation*, Cambridge, MIT Press.

Griffin, K. B., 1972, 'Pearson and the Political Economy of Aid', in T. J. Byres, ed., *Foreign Resources and Economic Development*, London: Frank Cass.

Hagen, E. E., 1962, *On the Theory of Social Change*, Homewood: Dorsey Press.

Hagen, E. E., 1968, 1975, *The Economics of Development*, Homewood: Richard D. Irwin.

Higgins, B., 1968, *Economic Development*, New York: W. W. Norton.

Higgins, B., 1973, 'Book Reviews of Dualistic Economic Development: Theory and History', *Journal of Economic Literature*, Vol. 11, No. 4.

Hill, P., 1968, 'The Myth of the Amorphous Peasantry: A Northern Nigerian Case Study', *Nigerian Journal of Economic and Social Studies*, Vol. 10, No. 2.

Kindleberger, C. P., 1965, *Economic Development*, New York: McGraw-Hill.

Knight, F., 1941, 'Anthropology and Economics', *Journal of Political Economy*, Vol. 49, No. 2.

MacDougall, G. D. A., 1960, 'The Benefits and Costs of Private Investment from Abroad: A Theoretical Approach', *Economic Record*, March.

Maddison, A., 1971, *Class Structure and Economic Growth: India and Pakistan Since the Moghuls*, New York: Norton.

Marx, K., 1904, *A Critique of Political Economy*, trans. N. I. Stone, Chicago: Kerr and Co.

Meier, G. M., 1970, *Leading Issues in Economic Development*, New York: Oxford University Press.

Meier, G. M. and Baldwin, R. E., 1957, *Economic Development: Theory, History, Policy*, New York: John Wiley.

Merton, R. K., 1972, 'Insiders and Outsiders: A Chapter in the Sociology of Knowledge', *The American Journal of Sociology*, Vol. 78, No. 1.

Mikesell, R. F., ed., 1962, *U.S. Private and Government Investment Abroad*, Eugene: University of Oregon Books.

Morgan, T., 1975, *Economic Development: Concept and Strategy*, New York: Harper and Row.

Müller, R., 1973, 'The Multinational Corporation and the Underdevelopment of the Third World', in Charles K. Wilber, ed., *The Political Economy of Development and Underdevelopment*, New York: Random House.

Myrdal, G., 1957, *Economic Theory and Underdeveloped Countries*, London: Gerald Duckworth.

Myrdal, G., 1968, *Asian Drama: An Inquiry into the Poverty of Nations*, 3 vols., Middlesex: Penguin.

Nafziger, E. W., 1975, 'Class, Caste and Community of South Indian Industrialists: An Examination of the Horatio Alger Model', *Journal of Development Studies*, Vol. 11, No. 4.

Nafziger, E. W. and Richter, W. L., 1976, 'Biafra and Bangladesh: The Political Economy of Secessionist Conflict', *Journal of Peace Research*, Vol. 13, No. 2.

O'Brien, D. C., 1972, 'Modernization, Order, and the Erosion of a Democratic Ideal: American Political Science 1960–70', *Journal of Development Studies*, Vol. 8, No. 4.

Prebisch, R., 1962, 'The Economic Development of Latin America and its Principal Problems', *Economic Bulletin for Latin America*, Vol. 7, No. 1.

Rostow, W. W., 1971, *The Stages of Economic Growth: A Non-Communist Manifesto*, Cambridge: University Press.

Seers, D., 1963, 'The Limitations of the Special Case', *Bulletin of the Oxford Institute of Economics and Statistics*, Vol. 25.

Singer, H. W., 1950, 'The Distribution of Gains Between Investing and Borrowing Countries', *American Economic Review*, Vol. 40, No. 2.

Thorner, D. and Thorner, A., 1972, *Land and Labour in India*, Bombay: Asia Publishing House.

Weisskopf, T. E., 1972, 'Capitalism, Underdevelopment and the Future of the Poor Countries', in Jagdish N. Bhagwati, ed., *Economics and World Order from the 1970's to the 1990's*, New York: Macmillan.

Modernization, Order, and the Erosion of a Democratic Ideal:

AMERICAN POLITICAL SCIENCE 1960-70

*Donal Cruise O'Brien**

INTRODUCTION

Staughton Lynd, writing from the frontiers of the American New Left, has recently drawn attention to the excessive optimism of radical 'theorists of corporate liberalism' who 'made the implicit assumption that capitalism in the United States would not turn to overt authoritarianism'. The political events of recent years have exposed the misguided thinking behind such an assumption: and the consequences of this miscalculation on the Left, he argues, may be disastrous. Lynd compares the prevalent view on the New Left, that 'the main enemy (is) not the reactionary right, but the liberal center', with the notoriously short-sighted tactical positions of the German Communist Party in the 1930s [*Lynd 1969, pp. 71–2*]. The comparison is certainly not wholly persuasive, but Lynd is on solid ground when he points to the erosion of liberal political values in America over the past decade, and to the emergence of an increasingly explicit authoritarianism. These latter trends are traced below in the writings of American political scientists, which give one indication of changes in official ideology. The argument is that the previously unquestioned political ideal of 'democracy' is in the process of being replaced by another ideal, that of 'order'.

Democracy as an effective modern political ideal appears to rest ultimately on some form of institutionalised tension between bureaucracy and popular influence in government: a balance of authority and liberty. In ideal terms at least, this may be held to be as true of Lenin's 'democratic centralism' as it is of capitalist electoral democracy, and even some of the vicissitudes of the modern Chinese state appear to reflect a working out of this same fundamental tension. The problem is a very general one, the

* Lecturer in Politics, School of Oriental and African Studies, University of London. Author's thanks to Michael Lipton for valuable comments.

49

balance always precarious: the argument of this paper is that the balance in America over the past decade has been increasingly weighted on the side of authority, hierarchy, and bureaucratic order. Political scientists in their writings reflect this change. A gradual loss of faith in liberty, in popular representation, has been accompanied and justified by a bleak appraisal of the governed masses, whose unrestrained political impulses are seen to lead to instability and even chaos. The need for restraint, for control from above, has been accompanied by a reassessment of those polities which have achieved hierarchical political order, and in particular to a new and more positive view of the political achievements of Soviet communism.

The subject matter through which these themes will be traced is that of the American political science literature on modernization. That is to say that the argument will be based on the scholarly literature of 'comparative politics', concerned with the post-colonial states of Africa, Asia and Latin America. (The terminology used by these political scientists—'modernization', 'political development', 'nation-building', for example—is adopted in this article merely to reflect the outlook of the authors cited.) The teleological quality of this literature serves to illustrate very clearly the shift from 'democracy' to 'order' as a political goal and ideal. Such changing normative perspectives, over the past ten years, are then related to patterns of contemporary political events.

Three major dimensions of political change are regarded as important in explaining the scholar's growing emphasis on the priority of order. First, the highly unstable politics of much of the underdeveloped world: it must be clearly recognized that the problem of order in the new states is not an invention of American political science, although the terms in which the problem is seen demand further explanation. Second, the change in emphasis of official United States policy towards underdeveloped countries, moving from an initial and timidly reformist phase to one of undisguised conservatism and counter-revolutionary containment. Third, in the domestic politics of the United States, a pattern of instability and violence which gives more urgent meaning to the theme of political order.

A concern to identify changing trends in scholarly thinking leads to certain problems of method and evidence, which should at least be mentioned before proceeding to the main argument. American studies in comparative politics, although remarkably homogeneous in dominant ideas, do include significant differences of opinion (and of subtle emphasis) at any one time. Changes over time are also blurred insofar as some scholars continue to propose well established views while others break new ground. The aim here is to be reasonably inclusive in approaching the comparative literature, but to focus above all on those political scientists who have enjoyed a wide professional influence, and on those who have made important original statements. Quotation is used extensively to give a reasonably precise indication of the views of particular scholars, so far as possible avoiding the temptation to paraphrase tendentiously. Selective quotation of course has its own dangers, and as applied here it may seem to suggest an almost staggering banality of received ideas in the political science profession. The reader who is unfamiliar with the writings cited, and who suspects this banality to be contrived in presentation here, is recommended to look to the sources himself. Particular attention is devoted to the leading members of the Social Science Research

Council (SSRC) ten-man Committee on Comparative Politics,* a group which has been very important in assuring a high degree of theoretical cohesion in the study of political modernization. Four major individual scholars are dealt with in some detail—Gabriel Almond, Lucian Pye, Samuel Huntington (all members of the Committee on Comparative Politics) and Fred Riggs. Many other scholars are cited, some within the dominant American tradition and a few outside: in the dominant tradition, wide reading shows how few original ideas are generated outside of a narrow professional elite.

THE MODEL OF THE MODERN

'The political scientist who wishes to study political modernization in the non-Western areas will have to master the model of the modern, which in turn can only be derived from the most careful empirical and formal analysis of the functions of modern Western polities.' *Gabriel Almond.*

Political modernity is representative democracy, and the practical achievement of the democratic ideal has reached its highest point in the United States of America. The process of modernization, in less advanced areas of the world, is therefore very simply to be understood as one of 'transition' in which backward polities will grow increasingly to resemble the American model. These were the confident assumptions of American political scientists concerned with modernization, at the outset of the 1960s. They were in particular the assumptions of Gabriel Almond, the most influential and the most theoretically sophisticated of these scholars. Almond indeed still holds to these basic beliefs, if in somewhat modified form, although their plausibility, and his influence on younger scholars, have declined over the intervening years.

The study of the politics of the 'developing areas' of Asia, Africa and Latin America, has been the work above all of scholars from the United States. Their interest in these areas dates from the 1950s, when a number of exploratory case studies were carried out in particular countries, and above all from 1960. The international political background to this new interest is of course that of the nationalist movements in colonial territories, the achievement of independence from European colonial rule, the creation of a great number of new states. Comparative politics could enrich its subject matter with a range of new material to complement its traditional concern with the study of Eastern and Western Europe, and of the United States. There was quite simply more to study, and political scientists could look with enthusiasm to the scientific and career possibilities offered by the study of new and exotic areas. There were also other reasons, more directly concerned with the exercise of United States power, as Almond recognized in 1960: 'Even in the absence of [this] compelling scientific justification for broadening the scope of comparative politics, practical policy motives have forced the modern political scientist to concern himself with the whole scope of political systems which exist in

---

* The committee was established in 1954. The academic members in 1971 were as follows: Gabriel Almond (from 1954, Chairman 1954–63); Leonard Binder (1962–); Philip Converse (1967–); Samuel Huntington (1967–); Joseph La Palombara (1958–); Lucian Pye (1954–, Chairman 1963–); Sidney Verba (1962–); Robert Ward (1958–); Myron Weiner (1962–); Aristide Zolberg (1967–).

the modern world' [*Almond and Coleman, 1960, p. 10*]. National independence for colonial territories reflected the final erosion of Western European dominance, and the resulting competition for influence between the two great Cold War powers could not but involve the 'modern' (American) political scientist.

The importance of Almond's ideas, outlined in his very influential 'Introduction' to *The Politics of the Developing Areas* [*Almond and Coleman 1960*] lies partly in a recognition of the need for empirical political research in the new states. 'Area Studies' had indeed already found financial support and an institutional position in several American universities, but Almond was able to communicate a new enthusiasm for comparative political reasearch among young scholars. His importance also of course lies partly in his preoccupation with the 'Western' model as a goal for developing polities. But American studies of the 1950s had frequently expressed this concern, and a great many words had been written on the pressing question of 'prospects for democracy' in a range of contexts. Almond's decisive contribution was to give a new coherence to these concerns in political science, through his elaboration of theoretical guidelines for comparative empirical research. The cogency of this comparative theory, and its claim to general applicability across the range of existing political systems, helped to earn it immediate and widespread acceptance. Such acceptance was all the more ready as the theoretical statement included an intricate reiteration of some generally held scholarly assumptions, and as these assumptions in turn reflected a complacent public opinion in the United States. The influence of Almond's views was reinforced through his position as Chairman (1954–63) of the SSRC Committee on Comparative Politics. The scholarly prestige and institutional eminence of the Committee's ten academic members, the conferences which it arranged and the research which it planned and funded, all served the diffusion of the new approach to comparative political studies.

Almond's new theoretical scheme did draw on a range of previous authorities in sociology and political science: in purely theoretical terms, his innovation is a limited one, as he freely acknowledges. From Talcott Parsons [*1951*] he derived the 'pattern variables' (notably the three dichotomies of universalism-particularism, achievement-ascription, specificity-diffuseness) through which the modern and traditional types of social system could be distinguished and compared. From David Easton [*1953*] the input–output model of the political system as a structure of interdependent parts, performing a minimal range of identical functions in all polities from the most primitive to the most advanced. And from the behavioural school of American political science, the emphasis on formal rigour in empirical methods and on the need to relate such empirical work to theoretical concerns.

There was much attraction in the very ambition of this scheme, its apparent capacity to give a basic orientation to the researcher confronted by new and bewildering political patterns. The political value preferences which accompanied the theoretical statement appear to have been too well incorporated to a prevalent scholarly mood even to have given rise to comment in the early 1960s. Almond's schema for comparative political research has none the less been much criticized in the United States in recent years, both for its claims to theoretical validity and to empirical

applicability. Some have commented on the irony of the fact that structural 𝕂
functionalism was adopted with enthusiasm by political scientists at a
time when it was under increasing challenge in the disciplines where it
originated [*Huntington, 1971, p. 308*]. Others have questioned the claim
of Almond's scheme to universal applicability. Dankwart Rustow, for
example, suggests that the crucial distinction between the making,
adjudication, and application of rules is no more than a gloss on the
traditional 'Western' distinction of legislature, executive and judiciary:
this trio frequently remaining impossible to disentangle in studying the
workings of non-western political systems. Rustow concludes that
'Almond laudably sent Western students of politics off to study the
non-West, but regrettably he sent them off with a conceptual baggage far
more distinctively Western than he realized' [*Rustow 1968, p. 43*]. By the
late 1960s, it seemed that Almond's influence was felt more strongly
outside the United States (see, e.g., Leys [*1969*]) than within.

These and other criticisms have to some extent been dealt with by
Almond in subsequent works, where he has further elaborated and refined
his ideas of 1960. Yet on the fundamental points he is unrepentant: as do
the leading structural-functional sociologists, he simply denies a static or
equilibrium bias, arguing that his functionalism emphasizes the inter-
dependence of parts, not their harmony. The parts appear to be sufficiently
harmonious, nonetheless, to permit a continued use of organic and
mechanical metaphors in describing the workings of the political system
[*Almond and Powell 1966, pp. 12, 13, 19*]. His evolutionary view of political
change is retained, and if possible indeed reinforced, in a series of later
studies. Equilibrium and evolution are the core assumptions of Almond's
brand of conservative liberalism. The character of these subsequent studies,
and of related work by other scholars who shared his liberal optimism,
may be worth consideration in some detail, especially insofar as an end
point of the process of political modernization is identified, and means
specified by which 'transitional' polities can hope to move in this direction.

The model of the modern has been clearly outlined in two works which
Almond co-authored in the early 1960s: *The Civic Culture* [*1963*], with
Sidney Verba; and *Comparative Politics: a Developmental Approach* [*1965*]
with G. Bingham Powell. In classic functional terms, this polity is characterised by a high degree of structural differentiation; also by a secular
political culture, with 'open, bargaining attitudes' and a pragmatic reticence
towards ideological movements; and finally by the autonomy of sub-
systems within the system as a whole. This third characteristic serves the
useful purpose of distinguishing clearly between communist and democratic
forms of industrial modernity, with sub-system autonomy referring to the
'pluralism' of groups and associations which American political science
has long seen as the effective basis of the democratic process in the United
States. Secular political culture, although seen as the counterpart of a
differentiated structure, again departs from the relative ideological
neutrality of the latter concept. It can be no great surprise to learn that
'rational, analytical, empirical' secularisation has reached its fullest
expression in the 'civic' political cultures of Great Britain and above all of
the United States. The idealized version of modernity has an American
face, and Almond's well articulated model may perhaps serve as another
reminder of the potential propaganda value of political classifications
drawn in terms of ideal type polarities. This ideal type is in effect the end

of history, the terminal station at which the passengers to modernization can finally get out and stretch their legs.

The means by which the journey is to be accomplished follow logically enough, and are the subject of general consensus among American political scientists. A combination of cultural diffusion and political tutelage will enable the modern polities to pass on their gifts to the transitional systems: in this dual process the political elites of the transitional states have a crucial role. Political leaders in the 'non-Western world' have their own commitment to this task: 'Though they cannot fully understand the subtle balances of the democratic polity and the nuances of the civic culture, they tend to acknowledge their legitimacy.' [*Almond and Verba 1965, p. 4*]. The confused but touching faith of the loyal native clerk. In this perspective, the difficulty that the modernized elite faces is then that 'the vast majority remains tied to the rigid, diffuse, and ascriptive patterns of tradition' [*Almond and Powell 1966, p. 72*]. Even at the mass level, however, the aspiration to Western modernity is held to exist. This is a conviction which Almond shares with many other American social scientists, notably those of the 'social process' school such as Daniel Lerner and Karl Deutsch [*Lerner 1958; Deutsch 1961*]. It is left to the heretical voice of Barrington Moore to suggest that 'there is no evidence that the mass of the population anywhere has wanted an industrial society, and plenty of evidence that they did not' [*Moore 1966, p. 50*]. Almond does acknowledge that the political dimensions of modernity pose special problems. He notes that the 'voyage towards democracy and welfare' will be 'long and uncertain', but he has no doubt that the vessel will come to port [*Almond and Powell 1966, p. 338*]. Some other American scholars even as early as 1960, had their reservations on the seaworthiness of the relevant ships of state (MIT Study Group in Welch [*1967*]). But Almond retains an unshakable faith in the outcome: technological change, international cooperation, the diffusion of a world culture of modernity, all must have their cumulative impact. Genuinely democratic political processes cannot be achieved in the immediate future but 'in the new and modernizing nations of Asia, Africa and Latin America, the processes of enlightenment and democratization will have their inevitable way' [*Almond, 1970, p. 232*]. David Apter [*1965, p. 38*], only somewhat more guardedly, holds it as 'an article of faith' that in new states 'the long term prognosis for democracy is hopeful'. Edward Shils [*1962*] and Seymour Martin Lipset [*1963*] also stress the relevance of the American model as a goal for 'transitional' polities. And Karl Deutsch [*1969*] in a general study of new states maintains a hopeful view on the future of government by popular consent.

The benign optimism of this view of the world, shared by so many scholars of Almond's generation, has not gained plausibility with the events of the past decade. The general acceptance of such ideas in the early 1960s is indeed only fully comprehensible against the political background in which Almond's major statements were formulated. Almond himself explained the achievements of the Committee on Comparative Politics partly with reference to 'the missionary and Peace Corps mood that swept the students and intellectuals of this country during the 1950s and early 1960s' [*Almond, 1970, p. 21*]. Peace Corps, Alliance for Progress, the reformist foreign policy declarations of the Kennedy administration, the early 1960s were years in which the overseas objectives of the United States could be presented as a clean break with European colonialism. And in

American domestic politics, the Civil Rights movement may also have helped to establish the legitimacy of a liberal and reformist style of politics. There remained, of course, the strenuous competition for political influence with the Soviet Union, but even here the American interest was identified with a democratic and liberal alternative to communist totalitarianism. Commitment to democracy as a political goal for new states, especially where it was explicitly recognized to be a long-term objective, may have been understood in some quarters to mean no more than a strategic alignment with the United States. The validity of the democratic ideal, in the light of certain features of the internal politics of the United States, may have also given rise to scepticism, but there remains a significance in the terms in which the ideal is posed and the official policy justified. There is also a political significance in the contrast between the liberal optimism of scholars such as Almond and the more pessimistic prescriptions of their major successors.

POLITICS IN THE FIRST DEVELOPMENT DECADE

The trend of political events over the years from 1960, in most of the underdeveloped world, had little reassurance to offer to those who conceived the future of new states as a more or less inexorable progress to democratic modernity. The prevalent pattern in many of these states has indeed suggested that the bland evolutionary assumptions of modernization theory are becoming a mockery of the real dynamics of underdevelopment. It should be recognized that American political scientists have in many cases adjusted their ideas in consequence over the past decade. To adopt a medical metaphor, they have recognized an array of symptoms and made a new diagnosis, from which they derive a prescription which suggests that the ideal of democracy has little relevance to the patient's condition.

The symptoms, in broad outline, are familiar to any reasonably diligent reader of newspapers and periodicals over the past decade. Among such symptoms, the statistical data of economics and demography must first be mentioned for their political significance. Rates of economic growth, measured in terms of gross national product, have often been unimpressive in the developing areas. Rates of population increase, insofar as these are accurately measured, have generally remained disquietingly high—the most impressive growth rate in some areas of the world. There are of course significant exceptions, but political scientists have been forced to recognize the implications of economic stagnation or impoverishment. The salient consequence, in the opinion of leading American scholars, has been to threaten that rising material expectations will become rising frustrations, and that a climate of mass unrest will undermine the political stability of new states [Lerner, 1964, pp.vii–viii].

Frustrations among the governed are obviously seen to threaten stability insofar as they are directed against the ruling elite, a logical enough reaction where the political and administrative leadership continues to enjoy great material privileges in relation to the mass of urban and rural dwellers, all the more logical where the elite appears preoccupied with the accumulation of licit or illicit benefits from the exercise of power, and where it offers few valued services to the citizens. The material conditions of life increasingly separate elite from mass, and also town from country, in many of the new states. The apparent revolutionary potential of such a situation have been noted by one or two more radical political scientists [*Weiss 1967*; *Miller and Aya 1971*]. Others have noted that mass grievances often appear to find a readier outlet in sectional struggles of more or less advantaged elements of the subject population, struggles in which sectional elites continue to command mass support on a sectional basis. The examples of Biafra and Bangladesh, among others, suggest that mass involvement in politics may tend to the disintegration of existing state structures rather than to the replacement of one elite by another within the same state. Such struggles can be particularly bitter where the 'national' elite becomes identified with a segment or segments of the population, and where other segments are themselves excluded from the exercise of power or the allocation of governmental resources. Mass involvement may finally take the form of more or less disorganised or even anomic violence, in which the boundaries between politics and crime readily become blurred—especially so in the proliferating shantytowns of much of the underdeveloped world. In whatever form spontaneous mass activity presents itself, however, it is seen by most American political scientists as a threat to the new state structures, therefore as something which must be minimised and contained.

The emergent pattern of authoritarian rule in so many of the new states, the use of a range of coercive techniques in the suppression of organized opposition whether by 'single party' or military leaders, have again offered little hope to democratic evolutionists. Even for those who suggest a need for a period of 'tutelary' democracy under firm leadership [*Shils, 1962*], there can be few grounds to believe that present forms of tutelage are likely to leave the pupils with much faith in teacher. The political structures of many of the new states, despite the often extreme concentration of formal power at the political centre, do not seem altogether effective in the exercise of power over their subjects. A number of observers, in a range of contexts, have commented on the conspicuous weakness of political institutions in the new states. Aristide Zolberg [*1968*] refers to black Africa as an 'almost institutionless arena', and Reinhard Bendix [*1964*] in more muted manner comments on the inability of Indian governmental structures to assure the effective integration of local and national politics. The fragile connection of local and central institutions has recently led some political scientists and anthropologists to an almost obsessive concern with the informal 'patron-client' or 'brokerage' structures which at least ensure some communication between centre and periphery through a chain of dyadic links.

Institutional instability in so many new states, the weakness of political structures and the alienation of large elements of the subject population, have perhaps been most conspicuously displayed in the frequency and ease with which ruling cliques have been overthrown by quite small (and often ill-organized) groups of armed men. The pattern of the *coup d'état*, once thought of as characteristically Latin American, now appears firmly established in Africa, the Middle East, and in some parts of Asia. This pattern not only of course suggests the near absurdity of a 'democratizing' teleology, it has suggested the need for a whole new analysis of the politics of underdevelopment.

The new diagnosis of the politics of underdevelopment, which has been increasingly widely accepted in the course of the 1960s, began with a re-examination of the evolutionary assumptions of earlier modernisation theory. These assumptions, notably so in the case of Almond, had been formulated without substantial direct experience of non-Western political systems—which at one point were dismissed in bafflement as 'uncouth' and 'exotic' [*Almond and Coleman, 1960, p. 10*]. Given some of the symptoms of a circular process of political dislocation which we have briefly mentioned, it is not surprising that Fred Riggs, for example, should later put the question—'may not some "transitional" conditions turn out to be relatively permanent?' The notion that they represent 'a temporary stage between a particular past and a predictable future state' may prove delusory [*Riggs, 1964, p. 4*]. Samuel Huntington, similarly, suggests that the problems of political underdevelopment may tend to be self reinforcing, where 'society as a whole is out of joint', and where political institutions are 'incapable of mediating, refining and moderating group action' [*Huntington, 1968, pp. 190–96*]. Starting from this hypothesis, these political scientists have attempted to develop a new analytical framework to deal with the disorderly politics of underdevelopment. Huntington has suggested the label of 'Praetorian' society, referring to those situations in which popular mobilization, the level of mass participation in politics, tends to increase faster than the institutional capacity to absorb the new participants. In such a situation, he declares, 'social forces confront each other nakedly' [*Huntington, 1968, p. 196*]. More of Huntington's views below, but at this stage it may be noted that his Praetorian model is formulated largely as a contrast with the political situation of advanced industrial states, and that it offers limited assistance to those concerned with the internal workings of 'Praetorian' politics at any level other than that of very large (and often dubious) generalities. Riggs, on the other hand, has over the years elaborated a highly intricate conceptual framework for the analysis of what he terms 'Prismatic' political situations. His prismatic model is perhaps the most successful attempt to conceptualize the problems of political underdevelopment at a general level. The complexity of the model, not to speak of the author's rather forbidding jargon and taste of neologisms, make it very difficult to give even a clear overall impression of Riggs' views in a brief space here: for those already familiar with his work this would in any case be superfluous, and for those unfamiliar one can best recommend a close and careful reading of Riggs' articles, and in particular of the collection published under the title *Administration in Developing Countries: the Theory of Prismatic Society* [*Riggs, 1964*].

The basis of Riggs' theoretical position is by no means novel, indeed it derives directly in concepts and method from the sociology of Max Weber. He adopts a modified version of Weler's traditional and legal-rational ideal types, but to these he devotes little detailed attention. His concern is with the intermediate, 'prismatic' situation, product of the super-imposition of modern political structures on backward societies. Here 'the new formal apparatus, like the administrative bureau, gives an illusory impression of autonomy, whereas in fact it is deeply enmeshed in, and cross-influenced by, remnants of older traditional, social, economic, religious and political systems' [*Riggs, 1964, p. 15*]. This perception of a situation of 'formalism' is certainly not startling or novel, but the great merit of Riggs' work is that he goes on from such a near banality to examine

in great detail the characteristic internal logic of such a situation. In so
doing, he has succeeded not only in elaborating a new and brilliant
phenomenology of the politics of underdevelopment, but in suggesting the
possible concealed logic and substantive rationality of an often chaotic
and superficially meaningless political pattern.

[The prismatic model is one of a fragile political structure, based on a
governmental elite which is politically powerful (in the absence of
organized or judicially sanctioned restraints)—especially and above all
under military rule, but administratively ineffective (in the absence of
viable institutions). Those who run the governmental machine, the 'elite
operators' derive material benefits partly from foreign sources (aid,
investment) partly from licit or illicit revenues derived from state corporations, partly through the application of pressure on the more politically
vulnerable sections of the population.]

The effect of the economic activities of members of the governing elite,
preoccupied with consumption expenditure and with the maintenance of
clienteles, is not the increase of productive capacity but rather a 'de-
capitalization' and 'mining of resources'. The society upon which this
exploitationary structure is imposed is characteristically highly frag-
mented, a 'poly-communal' agglomeration of groups divided by language
and culture, by caste, by religious affiliations, by local allegiances, by
perceived differences of race and historical tradition. These social dividions,
combined with the wide gap between rulers and ruled, give rise to a situation of 'poly-normativism', a fundamental dissensus on goals and myths
which creates a climate of moral insecurity in which there are few restraints on individuals or groups in the pursuit of their interests. Duplicity,
cunning, and violence naturally tend to flourish in such a moral environment.

The administrative structure superimposed on this social situation, the
'Sala' model which Riggs outlines in the most intricate detail, tends to
reinforce or even generate community divisions. The Sala administration
is characterized by a more or less unrestrained pursuit of self-interest on
the part of administrative personnel. Formal administrative norms are
manipulated selectively to defend or advance these particular interests
('double-talk'), and groups of bureaucrats (often communally based
'clects') in such competition tend both to alienate the subject population
and (above all) to deepen hostility and fears between communities.
Corruption and favouritism ('administrative price indeterminacy') is
institutionalized at each level in the bureaucratic hierarchy, superiors
extracting payment from inferiors to provide immunity from the application of legal penalties for illicit procedures.

It is impossible (and unnecessary) here to go into the rich detail of
Riggs' treatment of the Sala bureaucracy, a world where little is as it
seems and where the vocabulary of crime ('extortion', 'bribes', 'protection') is often tellingly employed to deal with the underlying procedures of
administration. One should note that Riggs does clearly recognize both
that these general 'prismatic' traits are present in widely varying degrees
in underdeveloped countries, and that they represent a tendency which can
also be identified in certain cases even in the most advanced and highly
bureaucratized industrial states. The prismatic tendency nonetheless
remains very much more pronounced in situations of underdevelopment,
and as a general tendency it appears to be all too relevant to the analysis

of the political process in the great majority of new states—in black Africa, in the Middle East, and (perhaps rather less) in South East Asia and Latin America.

Riggs' analytical scheme already has been outlined at some length here, although not of course sufficiently so to give anything like a full idea of his views. In the context of the argument of this paper, it has seemed important to review his work in this manner for several reasons. Firstly, he may be taken to illustrate the point that American political science is capable of making an important contribution to a comparative under- standing of political underdevelopment, in which 'Western' ideological assumptions or naive political value preferences are no more than marginally significant. Secondly, because his work on the whole enjoys surprisingly little influence outside the specialized circles of public administration studies. The wider significance of his socio-political theory has been largely ignored, in part no doubt because his prose can be peculiarly impenetrable, but also because his analysis is heretical in terms of the long dominant orthodoxy of systems functionalism. The mechanical metaphor quite literally breaks down in the case of a system where inputs fail to be converted into outputs ('blocked throughputs'): nobody would wish to embark on a long journey in a prismatic motor car. Thirdly and finally, because Riggs provides the conceptual material required for a new departure in the analysis of underdevelopment, where more radical political analysts have often done no more than engage in polemics which replicate the naiveté of their conservative opponents. Riggs is virtually unknown on the Left, but what he has done is to give serious intellectual substance to Gundar Frank's influential slogan, 'the development of underdevelopment' [Frank, 1966].

The politics of newly independent states, the patterns of disorder which now appear firmly established in so many cases, do suggest a peculiarly destructive quality in the legacy of colonial rule. This has been recognized, in a variety of ways, by a number of sociologists and political scientists. Reinhard Bendix, for example, has suggested that [the dominant experience of our generation appears to be that the unanticipated repercussions of European expansion were effective enough to undermine or destroy existing social frameworks, but often not nearly effective enough to provide viable structural alternatives] [Bendix 1964, p. 301]. This general view can be expressed with reference to political or market institutions, as by Riggs or Huntington for example, but it is also and perhaps most frequently expressed with reference to systems of moral values. The tendency to moral anarchy in underdevelopment is now very widely seen as a consequence of the fact that the intrusion of the colonial system in traditional societies has proved effective in undermining established normative patterns but has left little basis for the construction of a new moral system. The fragility and non-durability of many 'charismatic' and other self-consciously regenerative political movements very clearly illustrate the depths of the problem.

Riggs' penetrating analysis of the dynamics of prismatic underdevelop- ment is not as yet incorporated within the dominant American political science orthodoxy (as represented for example by the leading members of the SSRC Committee) but his broadly pessimistic evaluation of the future prospects of new states is echoed in many recent studies. Those concerned with the political promotion of economic development have frequently been discouraged by the apparent absence of institutions with the capacity to take on such tasks. Barrington Moore, in his analysis of recent Indian history, discerns little impulse either to modernization (industrialization) or to revolutionary political transformation [*Moore, 1966, pp. 334–84*]. Stanislav Andreski (not an American), in a general and somewhat intuitive survey of the African political and economic scene, speaks of 'a trend towards impoverishment which cannot easily be reversed' [*Andreski, 1968, p. 22*]. Those scholars whose concern is with political stability rather than economic progress are often little more hopeful, at least in the short term. Aristide Zolberg's [*1966*] survey of problems of institutional order in five African states, for example, or Lucian Pye's [*1962*] analysis of the political and administrative system of Burma, suggest a profound post-colonial crisis of institutional and socio-cultural dislocation. The SSRC committee, in elaborating a schema of distinct political crises, which have been handled successively over a long period in the course of the historical development of the advanced countries—crises of communal identity, of governmental legitimacy, of institutional penetration, of organizational participation, of political integration and distribution of resources—have suggested the peculiar difficulties of new states where the crises are all appearing simultaneously [*Binder, 1971*].

The great majority of recent American scholarship is agreed on one basic point, that few hopeful prospects can be held out to most of the underdeveloped world in the absence of the creation of new and more effective political institutions. The precise character of these desirable institutions, as will be shown below, does nonetheless vary to a considerable extent with the analytical and normative perspectives of particular scholars. Within these differences of view, there does emerge one major common prescriptive assumption, that the new institutional order should be the work of political elites, able and willing to impose new structures on the masses from above. The ideal of 'democracy', of effective popular representation in the processes of government, is in this perspective in the short run not merely irrelevant but in effect positively dangerous. This is true in the first instance, of those who see economic development (industrialization) as the primary objective of new states. Barrington Moore, with his humane Marxist revisionism, none the less emphasizes the compulsive and coercive techniques required to industrialize under either capitalist or socialist auspices. The initial economic problem is to accumulate a capital surplus at the expense of rural producers, but 'behind this problem stands a political one, whether or not a class of people has arisen in the society with the capacity and ruthlessness to force through these changes' [*Moore, 1966, p. 338*]. Bendix, although from another (Weberian) perspective, similarly argues that 'the industrialization of the latecomers typically involves a relatively high degree of political initiative' [*Bendix, 1964, p. 201*], both to promote economic change and to control the popular disturbance which such change creates. David Apter also sees the early stages of industrialisation as the characteristic task of a centralized and hierarchically structured 'mobilization system' [*Apter, 1965*].

The proponents of the ideal of political stability, now very much the dominant school of American political scientists, have of course been particularly emphatic on the role of governing elites in the creation of institutional order. The 'political order' approach will be the subject of the remaining two sections of this paper, in which this approach is analysed in some detail and related to the international and also domestic objectives of the United States Government.

If prospects for 'democracy' were the dominant concern of the late 1950s and early 1960s, then prospects for 'political order' have been that of the more influential recent literature. The rise of this new school of thought can be traced in the shift in membership of the SSRC Comparative Politics Committee. Almond's successor as Chairman of the Committee, and holder of that office since 1963, was Lucian Pye, who has been a consistent proponent of the ideal of political order. Of three new membership appointments since that time, two (Samuel Huntington and Aristide Zolberg, both in 1967) have written major works on the theme of 'order' in the underdeveloped world [*Zolberg, 1966*; *Huntington, 1968*]. Nor of course is the shift in emphasis confined to the SSRC Committee: it can be discerned across a range of scholarly literature in the past five years, as will be shown below.

'Political order' is a vague enough slogan, and it is important to recognize the prescriptive (and analytical) variations which lie beneath this widely shared commitment: that is indeed a large part of the purpose of this section. There are nonetheless many common features across the literature, in the profile of such an order. These also will be dealt with below, but at this point it may suffice to say that order is seen to rest on 'effective' political institutions, which may or may not be formally democratic in character: in any case this question has been of declining significance. Order is imposed from above on the mass, who remain manipulable objects of government policy. Within this general consensus there remain considerable differences of view on the particular category of political elite most likely to create stable patterns of deference, on the precise manner in which the objective should be sought, and also on the benefits seen to derive from a state of order.

Order may perhaps most readily be recognized in looking at its opposite, disorder, the many symptoms of political instability and underdevelopment which have already been discussed. If there is a spectre haunting the world of underdevelopment it is very often that of Thomas Hobbes, the nightmare vision of a 'war of all against all' unconstrained by shared social values or by political institutions. And the human costs of political disorder are without doubt in historical experience usually very high: only the Utopian can place his faith in anarchy. Yet given the solid empirical basis for a concern with political order in the underdeveloped world, it does also appear that American political science has treated the problem in a characteristic manner, which has at least as much to do with the international objectives of the United States Government as with the predicament of underdevelopment. The official advisory role of so many political scientists, the close links between American universities and government departments, and the generally shared commitment to a national ideology, are among the frequently mentioned explanations for this scholarly perspective. Commitment to an imperial mission in these circles has involved a declining emphasis on the desirability of democratic politics in America's client states.

The rise of the political order approach may first be related to the 'counter-insurgency' objectives of the United States, most particularly in Vietnam since the escalation of 1964–65. The views of the New Mandarins of counter-insurgency have been very adequately reviewed elsewhere [*Chomsky, 1969*] and there is no need to go into detail here. The enemies of order, for these warrior priests, are clearly the enemies of the United States, and the United States Government is directly involved in dealing with these enemies. Lucian Pye, an expert in this area, refers to the important 'short run problems of protecting a traditional society politically and militarily from the calculated attempts by well organized enemies of freedom to use violence to gain totalitarian control of vulnerable societies' (*Pye, 1966, p. 128*). For Pye, a founder of counter-insurgency, the 'menacing' Communists are still the main enemy. This is not the view of the other major American exponent of counter-insurgency principles, Samuel Huntington. But Huntington has enthusiastically accepted the American Government's objectives in Vietnam, and suggested his own chilling solution to the Government's dilemma. Accepting Mao's view of the peasantry as the crucial force in guerilla warfare, he has suggested first the classical solution of a programme of land reform to win over the uncommitted, and then put forward the more novel proposition that the peasantry should be moved *en masse* to the urban areas. If you can't catch the fish, drain the water. The partial application of this latter policy in Vietnam, with the massive use of aerial bombardment to stimulate rural–urban migration, apparently led one of Huntington's colleagues recently to reflect that 'Sam has simply lost the ability to distinguish between urbanization and genocide' (cited by Ahmad [*1971, p. 198*]).

The American government's international objectives have of course shifted over the past decade, and the desire to defeat particular communist enemies in Vietnam and elsewhere has not precluded a growing concern to find a means of at least partial accommodation with the major communist powers. The political instability of the underdeveloped world is potentially dangerous in this context, as the major military powers become drawn into local conflicts which eventually threaten to become world wars. Robert MacNamara, while Secretary of Defence in the United States Government, reflected on the dangers of the fact that 'whether communists are involved or not, violence anywhere in a taut world transmits sharp signals through the complex ganglia of international relations, and the security of the United States is related to the security and stability of nations half a globe away.' [*Bernstein, 1971, p. 143*]. The danger exists that the major powers become overcommitted to their often volatile political clients, or blackmailed by these clients into positions which effectively threaten the patron's own interests. Lucian Pye speaks of the need for 'a viable international order', but then in a revealing metaphor argues that 'in our concern with "winning the game" we often forget that we must also help establish the agreed "rules of the game" ' [*Pye, 1962, p. 298*]. Given this concern for international stability, it is natural that political scientists should look with alarm on situations where 'international problems can be expected to remain entangled with those of governments too weak to control their territories or population' [*Rustow, 1967, p. 282*].

The masses of the underdeveloped world, with high material and other aspirations, and low levels of allegiance to governments which fail to meet these aspirations, are in this context seen as a great potential danger. One response to this perceived threat is to attack the unrealistic expectations: 'in the Congo, in Vietnam, in the Dominican Republic, it is clear that order depends on somehow compelling newly mobilized strata to return to a measure of passivity and defeatism from which they have been aroused by the processes of modernization. At least temporarily, the maintenance of order requires a lowering of newly acquired expectations and levels of political activity' [Pool. 1967, p. 26]. This frequently cited judgment is in fact unusual in its brutal clarity, although similar ideas are often enough expressed by American political scientists. More frequent, perhaps, is a stress on the need to create an international community of political elites, a 'world culture' in which modern (American) values become widely if not universally shared. The elites may then, with their often near total control of the media of mass communication, transmit some version of these values to the people at large: this is an important part of the process of 'nation building', whereby sentiments of loyalty and attitudes of obedience are inculcated in the masses. Nation states thus become the building blocks of a viable new international order.

The process of nation building, as it is viewed by most American political scientists, becomes a prolongation of the politics of European colonial rule. Lucian Pye, again, refers to the 'period that British power was creating peace and order throughout so much of the world' [Pye, 1966, p. 132] and remarks that 'now that colonialism is ended we see the United States and others through various forms of foreign aid and technical assistance continuing the effort to shape numerous loosely structured societies into reasonable facsimiles of the modern nation state' [Pye, 1966, p. 8]. This approach to nation building is frankly manipulative. There is little room in such a perspective for a policy which seeks to create a national community by reducing the gap between elite and mass, or which sees the diffusion of some form of democratic rights as a requirement of legitimate national authority [Bendix, 1964, p. 19]. American neo-imperial policy requires a close cooperation from those who rose to prominence under colonial rule, those who Henry Bretton in the context of Nigeria has aptly baptised the 'foster-elite' [Bretton, 1962, p. 56], and the price of cooperation is the maintenance of the material and other privileges enjoyed by the elite. The 'national' order imposed by such an elite emphasizes the need for obedience among the governed rather than any profound acceptance of the rulers. Political order will be built by and around the governing elite: American policy, within the framework of the post-colonial state, is based on the principle that the successful exercise of external influence requires a policy of unite and rule.

The absolute priority accorded to the achievement of political order has, among other things, led to a reconsideration of some of the other objectives emphasized in the past, such as economic development, social reform, and also of course (if more ambiguously) political democratization. With the steady attrition of American foreign aid budgets in the course of the 1960s, it is not perhaps surprising that ambitious economic objectives are discouraged in client states. Myron Weiner, in his studies on the Congress Party of India, has emphasized the connection between the Party's successful record in maintaining political stability and its more questionable record in promoting economic development [Weiner, 1967, pp. 2–15]. 'A high rate of social and economic change,' he argues, 'creates

new demands and new tasks for government which are often malintegra-
tive . . . the challenges of integration thus arise out of the new tasks which
men create for themselves' [Weiner, 1966, pp. 165–66]. Aristide Zolberg,
in an African context, argues in almost identical terms [Zolberg, 1968,
pp. 73–77]. The new consensus, stated baldly, is that economic stagnation
may be the necessary price for political stability. This price may be accepted
more readily by those who do not themselves have to pay, whether they
by American scholars or national elites of the underdeveloped world,
than those who do—the masses condemned to continuing poverty or even
progressive impoverishment. In the immediate, it is easy to demonstrate
that economic development tends to increase inequalities of social class
or of communal groups, and therefore to exacerbate political tensions.
One might readily concur with Franz Schurmann when he notes, in his
discussion of the dual objectives of national unity and industrialization,
that 'most new countries have discovered that it is difficult to attain
both goals simultaneously' [Schurmann, 1968, p. xxxvi].

Social reform, a goal which implies the curtailment of elite privileges,
has been viewed with increasing caution over the past decade. The exuberant
rhetoric of the early Alliance for Progress years has on the whole been
replaced by a concern for the destabilizing potential of such reforms.
In the context of counter-insurgency theory, this is logical enough. A
policy statement of the Freedom House Public Affairs Institute in 1967
noted that 'many types of reform increase instability, however desirable
and essential they may be in the long term. For people under siege there is
no substitute for security' (cited by Ahmad [1971, p. 201]. A differentiated
view is that of Samuel Huntington, who argues that (land) reform aimed
at the peasantry tends to have a conservatizing effect, while reform aimed
at the urban middle class (extension of political liberties) tends to undermine political order [Huntington, 1968, pp. 380–96].

'Democracy' as a goal for underdeveloped states has already been
dealt with above: at this point it may suffice to note that there do remain
important divergences of view on this question among American political
scientists. Myron Weiner, in his work on India, emphasizes the viability
of representative structures there, and in particular notes that the Congress
Party (now solidly based on existing elites) seems to preclude a successful
communist movement by providing institutional channels for popular
grievances [Weiner, 1967, p. 489]. Most other scholars prefer to see
democratic institutions as a long term objective, and in the meantime
demand no more than 'reasonable facsimiles' (the phrase is repeated by
La Palombara [1963, p. 60] and Lucian Pye [1966, p. 8]) of democratic
modernity in the underdeveloped world. The eloquent emphasis of many
recent studies has been simply to disregard the issue. Perhaps one may
leave the last word on the subject at this stage with Robert Ward, who
suggests on the basis of his research in Japan that 'perhaps only modern
societies with modern political cultures . . . are practical candidates for
democratization' [Ward, 1963, p. 596].

Order, institutions, elites, these remain the priority concerns of most of
the recent American political science literature. But there is disagreement,
again, when one comes to choose the institutions and the elites best
adapted to ensure political order—an area of shared concern, incidentally,
with Soviet analysts [d'Encausse and Schram, 1969, p. viii]. Many scholars
have looked first to the post-colonial administrative structures in this

connection. Lucian Pye, in his study of Burma, refers to the 'need to create the communities of modernizers that can serve as islands of stability in the nation-building process' [*Pye, 1962, p. 296*], and concludes that these communities should be recruited above all from administrative personnel (with their technical skills) rather than political ideologists. The various scholars invited in 1962 to the SSRC conference on 'Bureaucracy and Political Development' on the whole shared this emphasis, expressed there for example in an extreme form by S. N. Eisenstadt. Joseph La Palombara, in editing the proceedings of this conference, expressed the view of most participants: 'in many places, government is the only significant social sector willing to assume the responsibility for trans-formation. In others, the bureaucracy husbands the vast majority of whatever necessary professional, technical and entrepreneurial resources may be available' [*La Palombara, 1963, p. 5*]. The bureaucracy in post-colonial states, he concludes, is often 'the only sector of the political system that is reasonably cohesive and coherent and able to exercise leadership and power' [*La Palombara, 1963, p. 23*]. The view of bureaucracy as a guarantor of order has of course been criticized, and with devastating effect, by Fred Riggs, who demonstrates that the actual workings of the 'Sala' bureaucracy tend to exacerbate political tensions and promote political instability rather than order.

Military rule is perhaps the most unqualified expression of government by bureaucracy in new states, and there have been studies which tend to emphasise the positive results of military seizures of power in the new states. Among these studies, one of the most naive but also the most influential is perhaps that of Morris Janowitz, who dwells on the superior quality of military organization and above all on the values common in the officer class—nationalism, puritanism, an ethos of public service and a commitment to modernisation [*Janowitz, 1964, pp. 27–29*]. Even Janowitz, however, had some reservations about the ability of the officer corps to cope with the political tensions arising under a military government, and these reservations have been amplified by other scholars. Myron Weiner, for example, notes bluntly that 'the much vaunted organizational skill of the military has often failed in many new nations' [*Weiner, 1967, p. 4*], and Samuel Huntington argues that military rule is only appropriate in cases where the process of underdevelopment is little advanced. The accumulation of empirical evidence over the past decade has of course tended to strengthen the position of those scholars who pointed to the flaws in the bureaucratic model of political order, whether or not the bureaucrats be armed.

Breakdowns in bureaucratic order (among other things) have led some scholars to re-emphasize the importance of an 'open politics outside of the sphere of administrative operations' [*Pye, 1966, p. 21*]: this 'open politics' is best organized in political parties, and these parties are seen as a means to control the masses rather than to allow a popular voice in decision making. Parties in general, and single party systems in particular, have thus been widely identified as the most effective means of building political order on a popular base. David Apter, for example, sees parties as the key organizational medium of modernisation, as 'the microcosms of the new societies' [*Apter, 1965, p. 186*]. Samuel Huntington argues along similar lines, for strong political parties which can mobilise and organize mass popular support, for single party regimes which can effectively 'dominate social forces' [*Huntington, 1968, p. 432*]. The manipulative drift of this latter argument has led to an important re-assessment of the 'democratic' style of politics, which has implications for the developed as well as for the underdeveloped world.

'Totalitarianism' was of course a central concept of American political science at the height of the Cold War period, when it served to stress the significance of Western democratic liberties in contrast to a system of highly organized political oppression. Such oppression might be communist or fascist in philosophy, but the organizational principles in either case were seen as similar if not identical: government by a ruthless elite, enjoying a total monopoly of power and extending its control into every aspect of the lives of the masses. Some political scientists concerned with underdevelopment have seen the new states as threatened by the emergence of such a political pattern. Henry Bretton, in an early article on Ghana, sees Nkrumah's leadership in this light, and uses European fascist and communist as well as South African parallels to stress the threat to individual freedom posed by the Convention People's Party's claims to a monopoly of power [*Bretton, 1958, pp. 62–66*]. A group of scholars from M.I.T. in 1960 concluded that 'the process of moderniza-tion . . . sets the stage for a struggle between the alternatives of freedom and totalitarianism' [*Millikan and Blackmer, 1962, p. 90*]. Fred Riggs, having traced the pattern of negative development in prismatic societies, regards it as alarming that this 'is likely to pave the way for cataclysmic revolution and the emergence of a highly developed, but malignant totalitarian order' [*Riggs, 1964, p. 44*].

Riggs and others may continue to view such a prospect with alarm, but there are American political scientists for whom totalitarian patterns of order offer a viable solution to the chaos of underdevelopment. The most important and influential exponent of this latter view is Samuel Huntington, who maintains that in underdeveloped polities 'the primary need is the accumulation and concentration of power, not its dispersion, and it is in Moscow and Peking, and not in Washington that this lesson is to be learned' [*Huntington, 1968, p. 138*]. Power must first be concentrated in the hands of an elite, then expanded to assimilate newly mobilized social groups: only later, and then conditionally, may it be dispersed. This view is most stringently and unambiguously expressed by Huntington, but it is by no means unique to him (see e.g. Welch [*1967, p. 16*]). Lenin's revolutionary theses are thus in the process of incorporation to the received ideas of the more conservative variants of American political science. Huntington remarks that 'the truly hopeless society is not one threatened by revolution, but one incapable of it' and for situations of underdevelopment and political chaos he poses the question 'Is not the only true conservative the revolutionary?' [*Huntington, 1968, pp. 262–63*]. The Leninist revolutionary provides a moral and institutional basis for the reconstitution of political order. His heroic role is not in the overthrow of the old order (there is little to overthrow) but in the imposition of an effective new one.

This reconciliation with Lenin may be seen in an international context of rapprochement with the Soviet Union in a period when Russian warships could cooperate with American ones in searching for an American aviator shot down in the China Sea. The two super powers also had a shared desire for international order, and from an American perspective there seemed to be a diminishing concern with the ideological accompaniment to institutional stability. Behind this there was perhaps the assumption that one can fruitfully negotiate and come to terms with *any* government that enjoys complete control of its citizens.

China, particularly at the time of the cultural revolution, occupied a special place in the new perspective of American political science. Huntington could look with approval on the achievements of the Chinese Communist Party after 1949, when stable government was established throughout the area for the first time in a hundred years. But in his view 'the undoing of that government . . . came when its leader abandoned Lenin for Trotsky, and subordinated the interests of the Party to those of revolutionary renewal'. [*Huntington, 1968, p. 343*]. The superficiality of this interpretation of the Cultural Revolution as 'Trotskyism' is convincingly demonstrated by Schurmann [*1968, pp. 540–70*]. but the conservative 'Leninist' fear of any more or less spontaneous and ill-controlled mass involvement in politics is very real.

The Cultural Revolution has of course been widely interpreted as a quite selfconscious reaction against Leninist principles and revolutionary organization, based on a distrust of the elitist tendencies of party bureaucracy—for which the Soviet Union provided a negative model. Mao Tse-tung was apparently of the opinion that the masses must be allowed to struggle against these elitist tendencies. There was doubtless an important element of manipulation from above in bringing about this arousal, and the tactical struggles of particular leaders or groups are clearly an integral part of the subsequent mass politics, but the underlying strategic principle remains vitally significant. Mao's encouragement of open struggle against the party leadership was based on his view that 'the forces of society control the state, not the reverse,' and that 'any alienation between state and society will lead either to tyranny or to a revolt of the masses' [*Schurmann, 1968, p. 521*].

This view, and the trust of the masses which it implies, may serve by contrast to highlight the authoritarian quality of much recent American political science, with its increasing acceptance of elite control as a political norm. The Chinese experience is not concluded, and changes at present under way suggest a reversal of some of the trends set in motion by the cultural revolution, a possible incorporation of China to the 'international order'. But China's history since 1949 suggests something like a cyclical pattern, in which bureaucratic control and mass mobilization alternate as dominant political principles. And the periods of mass involvement (Great Leap Forward, Cultural Revolution) remain as strikingly original features of the Chinese revolution. The slogan of the Red Guards, 'Dare to Rebel' may then finally be set against the precepts of the new American political science. An Orwellian alternative, 'Dare to Submit' might be suggested as the rallying cry of conservative scholarship. The political tone of these New Mandarins is not, as Chomsky would suggest, liberal. It is frankly and explicitly authoritarian. The label 'liberal' might appropriately be applied to most of the influential scholars of the early 1960s (Almond, Deutsch, Apter) but not to those who dominate the latter half of the decade (Pye, Huntington). It is a dangerous and widely current mistake on the Left to use the epithet 'liberal' indiscriminately, as a political custard pie.

THE PARTY OF LAW AND ORDER

The emergence of political order as an ideal in the literature on under-development may be related not only to new perspectives on American interests in dealing with the new states, or of course to changing social and political conditions in these states, but also to changes within the United States over the past decade. Scholars in general are of course affected in their analytical and normative perspectives by events which take place in their own societies. Political scientists, more specifically, work in a context which is shaped by the media through which they derive a large part of their information on the politics which takes place around them. The world of academic political study, as has been remarked before, is thus often closer to that of political journalism than most scientists of politics would be willing to admit.

The 1960s, depicted as a decade of political crisis is the underdeveloped world, was a decade of increasing political tension within the United States. Patterns of political disorder in new states could the more clearly be perceived by observers who had learned to recognize the condition in their domestic political situation. A reciprocal influence, more important to the argument made here, seems also to have gained strength. Some of those who became preoccupied with remedies for the disorder of under-development also turned their attention to solutions to similar problems in America. In this latter search one can identify an increased interest in the achievements of communist states, and particularly of the Soviet Union, in the maintenance of order within their own boundaries. Recognition of institutionalised communism as a model of political order is one logical outcome of a process of 'disillusionment' with the workings of representative democracy in the United States, and it is that process which is the theme of the remainder of this paper.

'Let us get America moving again.' John F. Kennedy's words gave apt expression to the mood of liberal reformism which swept the United States in the early 1960s. The black sit-in at a segregated lunch counter at Greensboro, North Carolina in 1960, inaugurated a series of non-violent protests intended to win full civil rights for America's black minority. These protests involved both black and white militants, and for a time they enjoyed a considerable measure of official sanction within the Federal Governments. While the black problem was seen as one of 'civil rights', which could in principle be solved by governmental and legislative initiative, it clearly did not threaten the institutional structure of American politics. The period of the early 1960s was also one in which large numbers of the young people of America, students and others, were active within the Democratic Party and its allied organizations. The aim of such young people, working in Civil Rights organizations or even in the Peace Corps, was to give a full realization to the American democratic ideal. Belief in this ideal had been strongly developed within the educational system of the post-war period, when democracy shone brightly in contrast to the dark alternatives of fascism or communism.

This optimistic mood seemed very remote from the perspective of 1972. Disillusion with the partial and largely formal (legislative) achievements of the Civil Rights Campaign brought increasing emphasis on separatist and/or revolutionary politics in the black community. The emergence of selfconsciously ethnic politics in the black (and increasingly often in the white) communities may have served perhaps as a reminder, if such be needed, that tensions of the 'poly-communal' type are not specific to the world of underdevelopment. White youth went through a process of alienation from the Democratic Party, a process which accelerated after Kennedy's death but began before it—the foundation of Students For a Democratic Society (SDS) in early 1962 being an important turning point. Escalation in Vietnam, the rise of black militancy, and also the violent death of a number of reformist leaders, all served to create a climate among a larger sector of the better educated white youth of near total rejection of a system which perpetuated massive injustice within and outside the United States. Destruction and violence are the most conspicuous and also the most politically significant expressions of this change of mood. The series of 'campus revolts' which began with the Free Speech Movement at Berkeley in 1964, the series of black urban riots which began in earnest with Watts in 1965, were accompanied by a mood of increasing frustration and desperation as the 'system' refused to yield. With these frustrations went an increase in the level of mass political violence, for which the defenders of order were very often responsible. The riots of 1967 in Detroit (43 killed) and Newark (25 killed), and the police riot at the Democratic Convention in Chicago in 1968, may be taken as high points of this trend. Subsequent political violence, for example among the white Weathermen and the Black Panthers, appears overall to have been on a declining scale—at least among the forces of disorder.

Politicians and political scientists appear to have responded similarly to these disorderly trends. 'Law and order' as a slogan and a theme in American politics certainly grew in significance over the years in which 'political order' became a major preoccupation of American political science. From Goldwater's unsuccessful campaign of 1964, with a stress on the problem of 'crime in the streets' (largely a code for the various symptoms of black unrest), to Nixon's successful one of 1968 with its dominant emphasis on law and order, one may discern a rising and increasingly hysterical fear of anarchy in the United States. The response of the authorities to various forms of political protest from 1968 onwards was one of violent repression: the Chicago convention in 1968, People's Park at Berkeley in 1969, Kent State in 1970, Attica in 1971, and the police war against the Black Panthers, are some of the milestones in this development.

The reflex of the authorities, and in particular of the police and military, has been to shoot first and find a pretext afterwards. In a real sense, indeed, the authority of government in dealing with protest evaporated and was replaced by force. As Sheldon Wolin and John Schaar point out in their perceptive essays on the subject, the legitimacy of the state has declined in modern America, to the extent where 'order and liberty stand in fatal opposition' [*Wolin and Schaar, 1970, p. 90*]. The heavy hand of government none the less still enjoys the backing of the majority of the citizens, appalled by the demands and by the political style of blacks and white youth. Jerry Rubin, the Yippie leader, offers a dream of the coming apocalypse which is the nightmare of these solid citizens. First, he says, the schools and universities will be closed down. Then . . .

millions of young people will surge into the streets of every city, dancing, singing, smoking pot, fucking in the streets, tripping, burning draft cards, stopping traffic . . .

Previous revolutions aimed at the seizure of the state's highest authority, followed by the take-over of the means of production. The Youth International revolution will begin with the mass breakdown of authority, mass rebellion, total anarchy in every institution in the Western world. Tribes of longhairs, blacks, armed women, workers, peasants, and students will take over [*Rubin, 1970, pp. 253, 256*].

Implausible in terms of the balance of power in American society, certainly, but this well publicized anarchist vision may have been sufficiently powerful to evoke its counterpart in a dream of total political control.

Alienation from the ideal of constitutional democracy is clearly not confined to the radical opposition in America. Wolin and Schaar point to the 'legal lawlessness' of those in high authority (Panther killings, prosecution of the Chicago Seven) and conclude that 'on all sectors of the political spectrum, there is a growing doubt that the liberal myth and logic will dominate the American future' [*Wolin and Schaar, 1970, p. 126*]. The importation of technology developed in Vietnam, in dealing with disturbances within the United States, is only one aspect of this development. The Pentagon bureaucracy now apparently includes a desk to handle domestic political problems [*Ahmad, 1971, p. 212*]. Established constitutional procedures may be disregarded as inadequate by those in power, with the support of the majority of the electorate, in the face of what they perceive as a fundamental threat to their authority.

Political science in the United States has a long tradition of distrust towards popular (mass) politics from The Federalist Papers to William Kornhauser [*1959*] and Seymour Martin Lipset [*1960*]. Fear of the unorganized mass rests on a bleak appraisal of humanity, as well as on a consistent strain of social and political conservatism. The consensus, that democracy can only run successfully where it is run by leaders, finds its modern expression in an endorsement of technological and bureaucratic elites. And political scientists share the bureaucrat's perspective in fearing the passion and unpredictability which may be unleashed if people escape control from above. Few would be so blunt, but most would agree with Samuel Huntington that 'popular sovereignty is as nebulous a concept as divine sovereignty . . . a latent, passive, and ultimate authority, not a positive and active one' [*Huntington, 1968, p. 106*]. Philip Selznick identifies the threat to democratic government as 'the emergence of the masses and institutional debilitation': more precisely, 'modern "mass" society runs the risk of exposing its institutions to subversive attack insofar as elites become insecure, mass behaviour influences politics and culture, and values become attenuated' [*Selznick, 1960, pp. xvii–xviii*]. More briefly, the danger to democracy is the people.

Secure elites and strong government are thus, in the United States as in the underdeveloped world, the political scientists' solution to social and political crisis. To re-emphasize democratic values would doubtless be implausible in a state governed by giant bureaucracies and elites which become increasingly inaccessible to those over whom their control is exercised. It is certainly at first sight more realistic to emphasize the potential of control which has developed with technological progress, even if the effectiveness of the control be undermined with the increasing distance and alienation of the ruled from their rulers. The political scientists' emphasis on stronger government in any case remains to complement the politicians' belief in law and order. The public is there to be manipulated. As Huntington puts it, 'the public interest is the interest of public institutions' [Huntington, 1968, p. 25], effectively implying that the public simply vanishes in favour of the elites which run these institutions.

Communist government, in this perspective, where 'the most important political distinction among countries concerns not their form of government, but their degree of government' [Huntington, 1968, p. 1], is an institutional model to command attention. A reappraisal of the political achievements of communism has indeed been under way for some time among American scholars, as already noted, with a marked decline in the use of hostile propaganda images of 'totalitarianism'. This shift should perhaps first be seen in the context of Soviet–American diplomatic activities: a common hostility to China in the cultural revolution period ('the greatest student movement in history' [Schurmann, 1968, p. 582]) could readily be justified by scholars of the political order school. Sino-American diplomacy, in the aftermath of the cultural revolution, can be justified in the same manner.

Institutional communism has become a factor of order in many western societies, as the insurgent students were reminded at the University of Nanterre in 1968, and it would clearly be absurd to persist with polemics against communist 'subversion' when the Communist Parties of Western Europe have become pillars of society. Martha Mitchell, wife of the United States Attorney General and articulate voice of the silent majority, gives a sure indication of the shift of consciousness at a mass level: 'there are elements worse than the Communists in our own nation . . . there are people in America trying to overthrow the Government by force. They are the American underground, both black and white', (International Herald Tribune, July 17–18, 1971). Mrs Mitchell's revised view of communism was reached rather earlier, and stated in a more complex manner, by academic analysts of communist politics. Zbigniew Brzezinski, for example, who co-authored an influential and strongly anti-communist study with Carl Friedrich [Friedrich and Brzezinski, 1956] declined involvement in a later [1965] revised edition of this work. His earlier work emphasized the importance of political indoctrination allied to a terroristic secret police in communist 'totalitarianism'. Later he refers to 'some major changes in [my] approach, emphasis, and judgment' when he concludes that their ideology has given the communist leaders 'a keen appreciation of contemporary social and political dynamics, an appreciation often lacking among their *dogmatically* undogmatic Western opponents' [Brzezinski, 1967, p. 3, p. 6] (italics in original). Philip Selznick dwells more explicitly on the lessons to be drawn from communist sources, first in developing a strategy to deal with communist subversion itself [Selznick, 1952], then in strengthening the elites and bureaucracies of corporate capitalism [Selznick, 1957]. For the insecure bureaucratic elites of the western world, there is clearly much to be learned from those whom it was fashionable to label 'totalitarians'. The modern may require remodelling.

'My idea . . . is "bureaucratic" in the sense that the party is built from the top downwards' [Lenin, 1944, pp. 447–48]. Lenin's elitist principles of revolutionary organization, set out most comprehensively in *What is to be*

Done? (1902), have been studied with some care by those who do not share his political goals. The bureaucratic view of organization, the stress for the need for an effective autonomy of the revolutionary elite, the manipulative tactics necessary to deal with a mass in the grip of 'false consciousness', these principles are those of a revolutionary army whose commissioned officers are drawn from the bourgeois intelligentsia with NCOs from the working class. Lenin came dangerously close to reducing Marxism to a set of political tactics: as has recently been remarked, 'from the rich and complex thought of Marx Lenin extracted above all certain recipes for the conquest of power. This was his strength, but also his weakness, as history has shown' [*d'Encausse and Schram, 1969, p. 31*].

For Lenin, the adoption of rigorous organizational principles by the revolutionaries was vital in overcoming the weaknesses of their political position: only organization could conquer power for a proletariat which often failed to perceive its own true political interests. The solution was centralized organization in the hands of a dedicated elite: 'we want the socialist revolution with human nature as it is now, with human nature that cannot do without subordination, control, and managers' [*Lenin, 1932, pp. 42–43*]. Yet it has become apparent with time that the proletariat's advantage need only be temporary: similar organizational principles may readily be adopted by its enemies. Mussolini and Chiang Kai-Shek, among others, read and learned from Lenin. In modern times conservative American scholars, such as Philip Selznick and Samuel Huntington, have done the same.*

The conservative or counter-revolutionary adoption of 'Leninism' leaves a few unanswered historical questions. If political order is the ideal, can one regard this as Lenin's achievement? The full triumph of elitism and bureaucracy might fairly be ascribed to Stalin. Samuel Huntington has a curious reluctance to acknowledge Stalin as a builder of political order. His tributes to Lenin are followed by a brief remark that 'beginning in the late 1930s, Stalin consistently weakened the party' [*Huntington, 1968, p. 26*]: little or nothing of the crucial fifteen years between Lenin's death and the great purges, when Stalin built the enduring monolith of Soviet bureaucracy (see Deutscher [*1949*]). Selznick seems more honest, at least with reference to the source of his ideas, when he acknowledges that 'in the case of Bolshevism, there is much evidence of a basic line of development, manifested in many different ways, from an early, inherently unstable Leninist phase to a more mature and stable Stalinist phase' [*Selznick, 1960, p. xvi*]. Where there is a difference, for Selznick it appears that Stalin is indeed the father of political order: 'the difference [lies] in the role of the masses; Lenin saw them as an active force, preparing the way for a quick rise to power. The Stalinists see their role as passive, always effectively controlled, summoned as occasion demands to strike, riot, or parade' [*Selznick, 1960, p. 256–57*]. And it is of course the latter view, bluntly stated, which comes close to the ideals adopted by many American political scientists. Back to totalitarianism: and if anti-

---

* Lenin's partial adoption by the authoritarian Right has of course coincided with sharp criticism of his political principles from some circles on the revolutionary Left. Rose Luxemburg's warning of 1918, that Bolshevik elitism would lead to the omnipotence of a 'red bureaucracy', has lost none of its force. Mao Tse-tung's reservations with regard to Leninism, already noted, are paralleled among the semi-anarchists of the New Left in advanced capitalist countries.

communist scholars in the past pointed to an effective convergence of fascist and communist political practice, modern exponents of political order seem to have come close to a position which would see the convergence in a more positive light. Manfred Halpern in a recent article has concluded that Nazi Germany would have to be regarded as the most modern country in western Europe in the 1930s, accepting the American political scientists' equation of modernity with prosperity and political order [*Miller and Aya, 1971*]. Adolph Hitler has not yet been adopted by American political science: his achievements may of course be held not to have stood the test of time.

The thesis of the convergence of industrial societies has long been held above all to imply changes in the communist world, where slowly rising affluence will be accompanied by increased demands for popular political participation. Gabriel Almond, for example, has expressed the belief that the Soviet Union must grow more 'pluralistic' over time, and in so doing will grow closer to the representative institutional patterns of the United States [*Almond, 1970, pp. 224–33, 310–31*]. A contrasting view is that of Franz Schurmann, that convergence has already proceeded in the opposite direction: 'the doctrines of "liberal" ideology in America have, in fact, adopted much of the *de facto* ideology of the Soviet Union, namely, that a benevolent state power dominated by technical elites, can insure peace and tranquillity for all' [*Schurmann, 1968, p. 521*]. One American political scientist, Samuel Huntington, has taken this latter view much further, and appears to see a solution for America's difficulties in the orderly political life of the Soviet Union.

Huntington's argument, while dwelling on the achievements of 'Leninism', is that the United States must overcome a handicap of political backwardness, a 'Tudor' institutional framework which has never been modernized. 'The United States', he argues, 'combines the world's most modern society with one of the world's most antique polities' [*Huntington, 1968, p. 129*]. The core of the problem is the weakness and disorganization of America's political parties, which contrast with the situation across the Atlantic: 'paradoxically, the form of political organization which originated in America was developed into a much stronger and (more) complex structure in Western Europe and was carried to its fullest and most complete development in the Soviet Union' [*Huntington, 1968, p. 132*]. There is still reason to hope that America may catch up, however, for Huntington concludes that changing circumstances may dictate new institutional patterns: 'the needs of national defence and social reform could undermine the traditional pluralism inherited from the past' [*Huntington, 1968, p. 133*]. A bright prospect indeed, of an orderly citizenry which has learned to accept political discipline, drawn up in regimented ranks to watch the Fourth of July parades.

The crisis of modern American society, evidenced on the campuses, in the black ghettos, and in the frightening crime and anomic violence of the great cities, has of course been greatly sharpened over the past decade by the many effects of the war in Vietnam. And it is among the strongest advocates of this war that may be heard some of the clearest demands for institutional change in America. Ithiel de Sola Pool, reviewing the Vietnamese experience, concludes that 'the agonizing political lesson that racks this country is that there has been a failure of our own political system. The intensity of dissent, the lack of public understanding of our national policy, and the divisions that rack American society today have thrown into some question the stability of government in the United States, the capacity of our system to govern effectively, the basic commitment of the American people to the payment of costs of our national goals' (cited by Pfeffer [*1968, p. 142*]). The same cry was heard from the French army of Algeria, at the time when the Generals wished to impose military rule in France—'stabbed in the back!'

Yearnings for a totalitarian order, which find partial expression in the writings of such political scientists, reflect a significant mood in America. Norman Mailer, a keener political observer than most political scientists, mused along these lines at the moonshot launching of 1969:

> It was a fit subject for Aquarius [Mailer] to brood upon. America was this day mighty but headless. America was torn by the spectre of civil war, and many a patriot and many a big industrialist—they were so often the same!—saw the cities and the universities as a collective pit of black heathen, Jewish revolutionaries, a minority polyglot hirsute scum of nihilists, hippies, sex maniacs, drug addicts, liberal apologists and freaks. Fantasies of order had to give way to lusts for new order. Order was restraint but new order would call for a mighty vault, an exceptional effort, a unifying dream [*Mailer, 1970, p. 56*].

Aquarius is by no means certain of the eventual triumph of those who have begun to think along these lines, and this caution must be shared by any observer of the rapid and often contradictory changes in recent American politics. But the authoritarian impulse is there, among political scientists as among patriot industrialists. Those who seek a radical transformation of American society from the Left clearly have more to fear than the familiar enemy of corporate liberalism with its political tactics of repressive tolerance.

The strength of the authoritarian undercurrent, beneath a formally democratic consensus, was underestimated or even disregarded by the American New Left in the early 1960s. Reaction on the part of established political leaders to radical politics since 1968, and the extent of popular support for 'strong government' in the face of organized protest, have been a sharp reminder of the fragility of democratic constitutional procedures. Indeed it may only be the recent relative quiescence of the Left which has prevented the full development of the politics of repressive intolerance. A large part of the purpose of this article, within the restricted domain of comparative political studies, has been to indicate the presence and some of the potential of American authoritarianism. The comparative study of politics, ranging across a variety of ideological and structural choices, tends to make explicit those normative judgments which may remain more or less disguised in particular case studies. In American political science the literature on systems other than that of the United States clearly illustrates the shift in normative perspectives which has taken place over the past decade. These writings may in the end be more informative about politics in the authors' country of origin than they are about the exotic areas studied.

REFERENCES

Ahmad, E., 1971, 'Revolutionary Warfare and Counterinsurgency' in *Miller and Aya 1971*.

Almond, G., 1970, *Political Development: Essays in Heuristic Theory*, Boston: Little Brown.

Almond, G., and J. S. Coleman (Eds.), 1960, *The Politics of the Developing Areas*, Princeton: Princeton University Press.

Almond, G. and G. B. Powell, 1965, *Comparative Politics: a Developmental Approach*, Boston: Little Brown.

Almond, G. and S. Verba, *The Civic Culture*, 1963 (1965 abridged), Princeton: Princeton University Press (Boston: Little Brown).

Andreski, S., 1968, *The African Predicament*, London: Michael Joseph.

Apter, D. E., 1965, *The Politics of Modernization*, Chicago: University of Chicago Press.

Bendix, R., 1964, *Nation-Building and Citizenship*, New York: Wiley.

Bernstein, H., 1971, 'Modernization Theory and the Sociological Study of Development', in *Journal of Development Studies*, Vol. 7, No. 2, January.

Binder, L. (Ed.), 1971, *Crises and Sequences in Political Development*, Princeton: Princeton University Press.

Bretton, H., 1958, 'Current Political Thought and Practice in Ghana' in *American Political Science Review*, Vol. LII, No. 1, March.

Bretton, H., 1962, *Power and Stability in Nigeria*, New York: Praeger.

Brzezinski, Z., 1967, *Ideology and Power in Soviet Politics*, New York: Praeger.

Chomsky, N., 1969, 'Objectivity and Liberal Scholarship', in *American Power and the New Mandarins*, London: Pelican.

Deutsch, K., 1961, 'Social Mobilization and Political Development', in *American Political Science Review*, Vol. LV, No. 3, September.

Deutsch, K., 1969, *Nationalism and its Alternatives*, New York: Knopf.

Deutscher, I., 1949, *Stalin: a Political Biography*, London: Oxford University Press.

Easton, D., 1953, *The Political System*, New York: Knopf.

d'Encausse, H. Carrère, and S. R. Schram (Eds.), 1969, *Marxism and Asia*: Allen Lane the Penguin Press.

Frank, A. G., 1966, 'The Development of Underdevelopment', in *Monthly Review*, September.

Friedrich, C. and Z. Brzezinski, 1956, *Totalitarian Dictatorship and Autocracy*, Harvard: Harvard University Press (revised 1965 by C. Friedrich).

Huntington, S. P., 1968, *Political Order in Changing Societies*, New Haven and London: Yale University Press.

Huntington, S. P., 1971, 'The Change to Change', in *Comparative Politics*, Vol. 3, No. 3, April.

Janowitz, M., 1964, *The Military in the Political Development of New Nations*, Chicago: University of Chicago Press.

Kornhauser, W., 1959, *The Politics of Mass Societies*, Glencoe: The Free Press.

La Palombara, J. (Ed.), 1963, *Bureaucracy and Political Development*, Princeton: Princeton University Press.

Lenin, V. I., 1932, *The State and Revolution*, New York: International Publishers.

Lenin, V. I., 1944, *Selected Works*, vol. 2, London: Lawrence and Wishart.

Lerner, D., 1958, *The Passing of Traditional Society*, New York: Free Press (1964 new preface).

Leys, C., 1969, 'Introduction' to Leys (Ed.), *Politics and Change in Developing Countries*, Cambridge: Cambridge University Press.

Lipset, S., 1960, *Political Man*, London: Heinemann.

Lipset, S., 1963, *The First New Nation: America in Comparative and Historical Perspective*, London: Heinemann.

Lynd, S., 1969, 'The New Left', in *The Annals*, March.

Mailer, N., 1970, *A Fire on the Moon*, London: Weidenfeld and Nicolson.

Miller, N. and R. Aya (Eds.), 1971, *National Liberation: Revolution in the Third World*, New York: Free Press.

Millikan, M. F. and D. L. M. Blackmer (Eds.), 1962, *The Emerging Nations*, London: Asia Publishing House (1st Ed. 1961).

Moore, Barrington Jr., 1966, *Social Origins of Dictatorship and Democracy: Lord and Peasant in the Making of the Modern World*, Boston: Beacon Press.

Parsons, T., 1951, *The Social System*, Glencoe: Free Press.

Pfeffer, R. M. (Ed.), 1968, *No More Vietnams?* New York: Harper and Row.

Pool, I. de Sola (Ed.), 1967, *Contemporary Political Science: Towards Empirical Theory*, New York: McGraw-Hill.

Pye, L. W., 1962, *Politics, Personality and Nation-Building: Burma's Search for Identity*, New Haven and London: Yale University Press.

Pye, L. W., 1966, *Aspects of Political Development*, Boston: Little Brown.
Riggs, F. W., 1964, *Administration in Developing Countries: the Theory of Prismatic Society*, Boston: Houghton Mifflin.
Rubin, J., 1970, *Do It! Scenarios of the Revolution*, New York: Simon and Schuster.
Rustow, D. A., 1967, *A World of Nations: Problems of Political Modernization*, Washington: The Brookings Institution.
Rustow, D. A., 1968, 'Modernization and Comparative Politics', in *Comparative Politics*, Vol. 1, No. 1, October.
Schurmann, F., 1968, *Ideology and Organization in Communist China*, Berkeley and Los Angeles: University of California Press (second edition, enlarged).
Selznick, P., 1957, *Leadership in Administration*, New York: Harper and Row.
Selznick, P., 1960, *The Organizational Weapon. A Study of Bolshevik Strategy and Tactics*, Glencoe: Free Press (first edition 1952).
Shils, E., 1962, *Political Development and New States*, The Hague: Mouton.
Ward, R. E., 1963, 'Political Modernization and Political Culture in Japan', in *World Politics*, Vol. XV, No. 4, July.
Weiner, M. (Ed.), 1966, *Modernization*, New York: Basic Books.
Weiner, M., 1967, *Party-Building in a New Nation: The Indian National Congress*, Chicago: University of Chicago Press.
Weiss, H. F., 1967, *Political Protest in the Congo*, Princeton: Princeton University Press.
Welch, C. E. (Ed.), 1967, *Political Modernization*, Belmont: Wadsworth.
Wolin, S. and J. Schaar, 1970, *The Berkeley Rebellion and Beyond*, New York: New York Review Book.
Zolberg, A., 1966, *Creating Political Order: The Party-States of West Africa*, Chicago: Rand McNally.
Zolberg, A., 1968, 'The Structure of Political Conflict in the New States of Tropical Africa', in *American Political Science Review*, Vol. LXII, No. 1, March.

Sociology of Underdevelopment vs. Sociology of Development?

Henry Bernstein

Once there was the sociology of development. Without necessarily having any more intrinsic coherence or unity than other specialisms within sociology (or the subject in general), a body of literature developed, bibliographies were compiled, conferences held, university courses on the sociology of development were established. This new field had hardly started its career of academic institutionalisation when it was subjected to aggressive attack: the sociology of development typified the 'underdevelopment of sociology' (Frank, 1967), the need to go 'beyond the sociology of development' was asserted (Oxaal, Barnett and Booth, 1975).

Several salient features of this challenge will concern us here. The first is that *under*development was now posed as the object of study more appropriate to the realities of the Third World, and as against prevailing notions of development and modernisation, which were held to be ideological. Second, underdevelopment was conceived as an active process rather than a passive or residual condition. The framework for analysing underdevelopment was that of 'the world system perspective', which sought explanations in international relations of inequality and domination/ dependence. As sociology lacks the concepts with which such a perspective can be constructed, recourse was had to an emerging political economy and economic history of the Third World in which the writings of Gunder Frank occupied a key place (1966, 1967, 1969a, 1969b, 1972a, 1972b). Finally, the association of underdevelopment of some areas of the world with the *capitalist* development of others suggested, though it was not defined clearly, some relation to Marxist theory. Despite (or perhaps because of) the uncertainty of this theoretical relationship the ideological thrust of a radical sociology of underdevelopment could lay a claim to the epithet 'neo-Marxist' (Foster-Carter, 1974; Hoogvelt, 1976).

SOCIOLOGY, DEVELOPMENT AND MODERNIZATION

How was sociology to find a place for itself in the new field of development studies which had burgeoned after the Second World War? One writer expressed scepticism as to whether the intellectual tradition of the discipline equipped sociologists to contribute effectively. In this view the interest of sociologists in problems of development was 'simply a case of sharing growing outside concern with the contemporary position of so-called underdeveloped peoples . . . there is no historical linkage of this new problem of "social development" to any of the three older sociological interests with which it might seem to have affinity . . . the interests in social evolution, social progress, and social change' (Blumer, 1966, p. 3).

Certainly it is true that the sociology of development which emerged has little intellectual unity or coherence, its object being a field of study given by the practical experience of underdeveloped countries and not by any shared theoretical categories. On the other hand, the failure to achieve a theoretically specified object of knowledge is hardly a distinguishing feature of the sociology of development relative to other specialisms in the discipline. Insofar as one perspective does bestow a semblance of unity on the literature of the sociology of development, it is that of 'modernization' and the formulation of 'models' of modernization. Contrary to Blumer, it can be argued that modernization theories both incorporate and adapt issues and concepts elaborated by the founding fathers of sociology concerning the themes of social change, evolution and progress (Bernstein, 1972).[1] In fact, the 1960s witnessed a significant revival of interest in social change and evolution by sociologists of the structural-functionalist school (see the articles by Bellah, Parsons and Eisenstadt in the *American Sociological Review* Vol. 29, No. 3, 1964; also Moore, 1963a, Parsons, 1966, Smelser, 1968, among others).

The Passing of Traditional Society by Daniel Lerner, published in 1958, was one of the earliest attempts to establish the agenda of a sociology of development. In commenting on Lerner's work, Bendix expressed succinctly the relationship between model and modernisation in this context. 'The great merit of Lerner's study consists in its candid use of Western modernization as a model of global applicability' (1967, p. 309). In the following review of the salient features of modernisation theories, our primary concern is with the mode of conceptualization they employ rather than with the substantive content of particular models of modernization, although some comments on the latter are made for purposes of illustration.

The destination: models of modernity

Modernization is by definition the process of change towards the condition of modernity. The social entity undergoing modernization may be a society, economy, polity or culture (or, as in personality theories of 'modern man', the individual is the unit of analysis). The categories of these forms of theorization can also be applied in the study of particular social or institutional spheres—the family, the city, the village, education, bureaucracy, the military, and so on.

Our first question concerns the source of what is modern. As modernization theorists have explicitly stated, the content of modernity is given by the experience of those societies which have achieved it, namely the societies of Western Europe and North America which combine industrial economies with representative democracy. To accept this statement of the historically given, however, would be far too innocent. The social content of modernity is not 'given' by a certain history, but is formulated according to the categories through which that history is appropriated and reflected upon in sociological theory.

Broadly speaking, modernization theories can be distinguished according to whether the concepts constituting modernity are formulated at the level of social structure, culture or personality. The first traces its theoretical ancestry to the evolutionism of Spencer and Durkheim, conceiving the process of change in terms of increasing societal differentiation and complexity. On the analogy of the division of labour, extended to all spheres of society, a modern society is one in which a wide range of specialized institutions and roles are functionally related through corresponding agencies of integration (Smelser, 1963; Friedland in Morse *et al.,* 1969; Chodak, 1973). The function of specialization is to increase the capacity of the modern society to respond to changes generated internally, or by the external environment, in ways that do not endanger social stability. An equivalent notion in economics might be that of the capacity to sustain 'balanced growth'.

Cultural modernization theories have as their object the sphere of values, goals, norms and attitudes. Their preoccupation with religious ideas reflects their inspiration by Weber's thesis concerning *The Protestant Ethic and the Spirit of Capitalism*. The central concept here, as for Weber, is that of rationality identified at the level of both individual social action and the organizational rules of institutions.

Personality theories have as their object the concept of 'modern man', a type of social actor equipped with the value and cognitive orientations deemed necessary for effective participation in modern society (Lerner, 1958). 'Modern man' is one who has the ability to fulfil the obligations of a number of roles in different areas of social action (job-performance, consumption, citizenship, membership of voluntary organizations, family, etc.). Various inventories of the desirable traits of modern man have been compiled, which differ according to the type of psychological theory employed. McClelland's notion of 'need for achievement' or *n. ach.* is the best known expression of personality theory (McClelland, 1961). McClelland makes it clear that entrepreneurship (sometimes more abstractly expressed as 'innovative ability') is the central *motif* of this approach.[2]

The departure point: non-modernity

What these various formulations have in common is that they posit models of modernity held to represent the product of a historical process in the West, which is at the same time a historical promise for other parts of the world.

Historically, modernization is the process of change toward those types of social, economic and political systems that have developed in Western Europe and North America from the seventeenth century to the nineteenth and have then spread to other European countries and in the nineteenth and twentieth centuries to the South American, Asian and African continents (Eisenstadt, 1966, p. 1).

(Social scientists) persist in using the term (modernization) not only because it is a part of popular speech, but also because they recognize that these many changes (in individual attitudes, in social behavior, in economics, and in politics) are related to one another—that many countries in the developing world today are experiencing a comprehensive process of change which Europe and America once experienced and which is more than the sum of many small changes (Preface to Weiner, 1966).

Conforming to the teleological character of 'before and after' models of social change, the process (modernization) is defined by its destination. In relation to the destination of modernity the departure point is the non-modern or traditional, a necessarily residual category. While this fundamental dualism—underdeveloped/developed, traditional/modern—is a conceptual currency standard throughout development studies, in the sociology of development it also subsumes a range of polar ideal-types contained in the sociological tradition and which perform a similar theoretical function: status/contract, sacred/secular, mechanical solidarity/ organic solidarity, community/association, and the pattern variables of Talcott Parsons (Hoselitz, 1963).

When the purpose, by common consent, is to promote a programme of modernization, there is a tendency to aggregate all that is *non*-modern, irrespective of the various types of *pre*-modern societies. This effect of definition in Rostow's concept of the traditional, for example, has been noted by Raymond Aron.

All past societies are put into this single category, whether they be the archaic communities of New Guinea, the Negro tribes of Africa, or the old civilizations of India and China. But the only feature they have in common is that they are neither modern nor industrialised (Aron, 1964, p. 30).

Reaching the destination: the process of modernization

The process of modernization is charted in the cumulative development of elements of modernity which displace non-modern elements. Various indices have been devised for measuring the degree of modernization, exemplifying an underlying method of comparative statics. 'On the basis of indicators $a, b, c \ldots$ developing country x in the 1970s corresponds to the stage of modernization of developed country y in the 1890s'. Whether put as baldly as this or employed implicitly, this form of reductionism is a pervasive one and explains the appeal of Rostow's stage model to sociologists of development.[3]

How modernization is to be achieved is a question that has vexed sociologists seeking to contribute to development studies, especially in view of the primacy given to issues of economic development. Moore observed some years ago that sociologists had failed to say much about economic development (1963b, p. 520), while Smelser and Lipset attempted to deflect the problem by suggesting that 'other sectors of the social structure (may) provide the developmental vanguard movement' in opposition to the view of economic change as primary which they attributed to 'the combined influence of the classic British model of industrialization, as well as lingering materialist assumptions' (1968, pp. 157–8).

The problem remains, however, and it reflects the lack of any concepts of social production in sociology. The classical social theorists were preoccupied with the disruptive effects of the industrialization of nineteenth-century Europe and how to maintain social control and stability in face of the destruction of those social institutions and ideologies that had previously guaranteed them. For them the intensity and scale of economic change were given and not problematic, as they are for contemporary development studies where the issue is how to achieve development.

Practically sociologists have tried to stake their claim not by questioning the content of the growth models of the economists but by suggesting that they presuppose certain social and cultural conditions which sociologists are equipped to analyse (Weinberg, 1969, p. 3). On similar lines Hoselitz, an economic historian, has questioned the *ceteris paribus* clause of the economic growth theories, stating that 'one cannot always proceed as if all other things remained equal; for often they do not, and it is the change in those 'other things' which is crucial (Hoselitz, 1965, p. 183; or in Smelser and Lipset's words, modernization in other sectors of the social structure—education or the polity are their suggestions—may provide the 'developmental vanguard movement').

This represents an attempt to switch from an exclusive focus on the effects of economic development to the consideration of its (non-economic) conditions.[4] One characteristic expression of this has been the preoccupation with entrepreneurship. Within the framework of an idealist conception of the modern economy derived from Weber—that is, the economy constituted by the actions of economic subjects related to each other through the market—some sociologists and anthropologists have sought to identify the social and cultural determinants of economic innovation. This type of analysis has often concerned itself with seeking in 'non-Western societies' cultural 'equivalents' to ascetic Protestantism as the ideational source of rational economic behaviour (Eisenstadt ed., 1968). Another expression of this approach is the construction of typologies of 'modernizing élites' or regimes as functionally 'equivalent' agents capable of carrying out the tasks of economic as well as political modernization (Lamb, 1952; Kerr *et al.*, 1964. The typological analysis of regimes has been one of the major themes in the political modernization literature, which replicates the mode of conceptualization and theoretical effects of modernization models in sociology—see Bernstein, 1971).

The model of modernity is non-problematic. It only abstracts from a historical process that has already been realized in the West. On the other hand, the process of modernization is problematic for the underdeveloped countries today, not only because they have yet to arrive at the prescribed destination but because of the possibility of 'breakdowns of modernization' *en route* (Eisenstadt, 1969). One way of conceptualizing such 'breakdowns' is to see them as the effect of a lag in the development of agencies of integration relative to the process of differentiation (Smelser, 1963), the circularity of which is a necessary effect of the mode of theorization employed (as well as reflecting a Durkheimian view of social disorder).

Alternatively, the category of the traditional can be elevated from its passive and residual status (that of the non-modern) to an active effectivity, representing 'obstacles to development'. This is clear in the notion of the dual society, the concept of a transitional formation appropriate to the mode of conceptualization of modernization theory. The fundamental dualism rooted in the polar concepts of modernity and tradition now takes as its concrete object the dual society, consisting of modern and traditional sectors. The various sources of dynamism (economic, social, cultural, psychological) are located in the modern sector, around which the traditional sector forms a recalcitrant hinterland resisting the penetration of modern organization and behaviour.[5]

Concepts of 'breakdowns of modernization', 'obstacles to development' and the like, reflect the assumption built into modernization theories that 'developing countries are infant or deviant examples of the Western experience and can be studied in terms of shortfall from a norm' (Nettl, 1967, p. 193). In this way the postulates of the modernization models not only prescribe a certain course of development but simultaneously provide a social pathology of the consequences of deviation from this course. Thus for W. W. Rostow communism is 'a disease of the transition' (1960, pp. 192–4). For Daniel Lerner the syndrome of rapid urbanization com-

82 DEVELOPMENT THEORY

bined with extensive unemployment and the poverty of shanty-town life reflects a breakdown 'in the "transition" from agricultural to urban-industrial labour *called for by the mechanism of development and the model of modernization'*. This breakdown is explained by the fact that 'the modernizing lands are societies-in-a-hurry. Emulating what the advanced Western societies have become today, they want to get there faster. Accordingly, they force the tempo of Western development. Even more serious, as a result of their hurried pace, *they often disorder the sequence of Western development'* (Lerner, 1967, p. 24, emphasis added).[6]

In the light of these statements it is perhaps not surprising that modern-ization theories have been attacked as ideological. Their naïvely enthusi-astic prescriptions add up to a celebration of the virtues of Western society: prosperity, democracy, efficiency, participation, growth with stability. Their message to the Third World is—'if you want to have what we have, then be like us, do as we do'.[7] To the extent that the professional ideology of development studies combines the ethics of welfarism with the technics of growth economics, radical critics have been able to retort 'Your models have failed'. All the expressions of concern, the aid programmes, the training programmes and technical assistance, the concentration of expertise in the applied field of development studies, have failed to make any impression on the standards of living and life-chances of the masses of people in the Third World.[8]

When one considers further that the major events in the Third World during the 'Development Decades' of the 1960s and 1970s have been the national liberation struggles waged in Indochina and Africa, and a systematically brutal repression of progressive forces in some of the most strategic countries of Latin America and Asia, the vulnerability of the development experts and their abstracted models to radical criticism appears even more obvious. Counterposed to the sociology of develop-ment there is now a radical sociology of underdevelopment which puts exploitation and oppression—and liberation from them—at the centre of its concerns. The nature of this challenge is the object of the next section of this essay, but before proceeding it is necessary to say something more about the ideological character of modernization theories.

Their specific *ideological content* has been pointed out clearly enough by a number of radical critics (Frank, 1967; Rhodes, 1969; Hilal, 1970; Bernstein, 1971, 1972), but there is another *theoretical* sense in which modernization theories are ideological which concerns the mode of con-ceptualization they employ and its effects. As has been demonstrated above, the constitution of modernization as a process by the concept of its destination, modernity, is necessarily teleological, and necessarily leads to circular reasoning.

This circularity is further exemplified, rather than being broken, by attempts to modify or differentiate the content of the concepts of modern-ity, tradition and modernization. For example, representative democracy may be waived in the model of the modern polity in order to accommodate a more abstract requirement of 'order-maintenance' (which permits the classification of repressive regimes friendly to the West as authentic modernizers).[9] Traditional societies may be differentiated in the quest for cultural 'equivalents' to the Protestant Ethic as the source of rational economic behaviour, or in terms of other specified 'predispositions to modernity'. In no way does this alter the procedure of conceptualizing the traditional as an effect of the model of the modern. As a final example, modernizing societies may be allowed to find different means of satisfying the functional stages of the model of modernization, but the legitimacy of these means is legislated by the model. The latter maps out 'the golden road to modernity' in general and is not responsible for those who get stuck on the journey or fall by the wayside.

This essential circularity is characteristic of an ideological discourse in the theoretical sense, that is, a discourse which is unable to *problematize* its object in order to carry out the tasks of investigation necessary to any science. The determining model of modernity, from which everything else follows, is itself non-problematic as it is already 'given' by the historical development of the West. This mode of conceptualization can only produce answers that are already determined by the way in which questions are posed, and in concrete analysis its effect is the fitting of facts to categorical 'boxes'. It is incapable of satisfying the theoretical conditions of investigation of an object of knowledge, and accordingly is incapable of producing any knowledge of the object it poses other than that given by its definition. In short, it is condemned to the closed circle of an ideological discourse from which it cannot break out.[10]

THE DEVELOPMENT OF UNDERDEVELOPMENT

The sociology of underdevelopment that has emerged in direct opposition to the sociology of modernization is inspired by a certain kind of political economy/economic history of the Third World, which the writings of André Gunder Frank have been most influential in establishing. Radical sociologists have had to go outside the theoretical tradition of their discipline to find the categories with which to construct a sociology of the Third World centred on the themes of exploitation and oppression. The distinctive feature of this project has been a radical revision of the content of the term 'underdevelopment' itself, the salient features of which can be summarized as follows.

1. It was necessary first to reject the linear evolutionism of the conventional models in which underdevelopment (or tradition) is an 'original state' from which all societies start in relation to the goal of development (or modernity). The 'original state' view has been concisely expressed by Hoselitz: 'If there are "developed" and "advanced" countries in the present they must have at some time been "underdeveloped" ' (Preface to Hoselitz ed., 1952). The reply of Frank was to say that 'The developed countries were never *under*developed, though they may have been *un*developed' (1966, p. 18). Underdevelopment is no longer to be regarded as a residual and passive condition, but is a phenomenon resulting from a particular historical process.

2. The countries of the Third World were actively underdeveloped in the process of the emergence and consolidation of capitalism as a world system. The original centres of capitalism established their wealth and their power through incorporating and exploiting other parts of the world. The primary accumulation of capital in the metropoles or centre was fed through a drain of wealth from the satellite or peripheral countries, typically involving their colonization, a 'surplus drain' which continues to the present day even if its forms may have changed, and direct colonial rule is no longer a necessary condition of this process.

3. Underdevelopment is therefore neither an 'original state' nor is it perpetuated by the 'obstacles to development' presented by tradition, but is the function of a particular position in the structure of the world system established by capitalism. The self-sustaining character of capitalist development in the centre and the reproduction of underdevelopment of the peripheral countries are parts of a single process.

4. This signifies that development has failed to take off, and cannot take off, in the periphery as the conditions of such a process—an autonomous accumulation of capital effected through the agency of a genuine national bourgeoisie—are pre-empted by dependence on and subordination by the capitalist centre.

5. Given the impossibility of national capitalist development within the world system (or outside it by autarchic means), the only way of achieving development is to 'disengage' from the system as the necessary precondition for those fundamental political, social and economic changes required to achieve 'self-centred' development (socialism in one country appears to be possible while capitalism in one country is not).

Within this framework variants on the basic themes are encountered (which partly reflect the different ways in which a Marxist terminology is applied). For example, with respect to the periodization of world capitalist economy variant forms of underdevelopment may be suggested as typical of different periods. These may be traced through stages of the development of capitalism (primitive accumulation—competitive capitalism—monopoly capitalism), or through a succession of dominant forms of capital (merchant's capital—industrial capital—finance capital). Different mechanisms of 'surplus drain' are suggested (sometimes identified with the stages of a periodization), for example, unequal exchange, repatriation of profits on investments by foreign capital, debt-servicing, and the accounting procedures of multinational corporations (transfer-pricing etc.).

There are also variant characterizations of the structures of underdevelopment, notably focusing on the dualism controversy. With respect to the latter, differences are often less significant than is commonly supposed insofar as both the views of the dependent formations as 'capitalist' from the moment of their incorporation into the world system (Frank, 1969a; Wallerstein, 1974a, 1974b), or as dualistic (Amin, 1976, pp. 22, 217–8, 271, 294), attribute the primary determination to the interests of (metropolitan) capital.

As a final illustration, there are variant explanations of the reproduction of underdevelopment—as an effect of surplus drain inhibiting the indigenous accumulation of capital, as the result of the 'distorted' structures of production and income distribution caused by direct or indirect domination by foreign capital, or associated with the inability of indigenous industry to compete effectively with multi-national corporations concentrating capital and advanced technology on a global scale.

None of these variants are incompatible within the framework of underdevelopment theory and the mode of conceptualization it employs. They appear as differences of emphasis, and are often combined in the same text (notably Amin, 1976a, which is a compendium of virtually every proposition ever advanced by underdevelopment theory, assembled in a chaotic manner). As with our review of modernization theories, we shall be more concerned in what follows with the mode of theorization characteristic of underdevelopment theory and its effects, rather than with differences between particular expressions of this kind of theory.[11]

Capitalism and the model of the central economy

Although capitalism is the central term which explains all—'Development and underdevelopment each cause and are caused by the other in the total development of capitalism' (Frank, 1969a, p. 240)—capitalism has been theorized remarkably little in underdevelopment theory. In the work of Gunder Frank capitalism is identified with commodity production, especially for the world market, a conceptualization that fails to establish the distinctive categories of the capitalist mode of production, and therefore the theoretical means for investigating and differentiating the historical epoch of capital. This has been one of the most consistent criticisms of Frank (Arrighi, 1971; Laclau, 1971), and the effects of Frank's notion of capitalism are expressed in his theses that 'monopoly capitalism' was established in their sixteenth-century colonies by the feudal kingdoms of Portugal and Spain, and that the essential structural features of underdevelopment instituted at that time have persisted to the present day.

For Wallerstein, who closely follows Frank, 'the essential feature of a capitalist world economy (is) production for sale in a market in which the object is to realize the maximum profit' (1974b, p. 398). The capitalist world economy is a 'historically specific totality . . . that has existed for about four or five centuries now' (ibid, pp. 391, 397). Its regional division of labour is the basis of 'a grid of exchange relationships . . . (which) comes about by the attempts of actors in the market to avoid the normal operations of the market whenever it does not maximize their profit' (ibid, pp. 397, 400). This reveals an idealist conception, derived from Weber, which sees capitalism as constituted by the calculations and actions of economic subjects ('actors') linked by the market.

The formulation of capitalism as an economy of exchange relations is also found in the work of Emmanuel for whom 'the main problem' of capital is not to produce but to sell, capitalism being 'a system of mercantile relations' (1975, pp. 70, 71, and *passim*). In these examples, the only categories made available for defining capitalism are those of commodity production, market relations and profit, none of which are peculiar to the capitalist mode of production and its *social relations of production*. That such categories fail to establish the specificity of capitalism, and therefore fail to distinguish it from other historical forms of commodity production and exchange, has been pointed out often enough for us not to labour the point further.

What seems to have attracted much less attention is the conception of advanced capitalist economies in underdevelopment theory. Their distinctive features are rarely formulated explicitly, as the main concern is with the predatory character of the centre vis-à-vis the periphery. However, 'since the peripheral economy exists only as an appendage of the central economy' (Amin, 1976, p. 345), the lack of theorization of the latter is a major lacuna. Nonetheless, underdevelopment theories do contain an underlying and pervasive image of the advanced capitalist countries as having achieved 'self-sustained growth', which provides in turn an ideological description of underdevelopment, as we shall argue below. Ironically the notion of 'self-sustained growth' is derived from the ideological arch-enemy, W. W. Rostow.

Fortunately one underdevelopment theorist, namely Samir Amin, has undertaken to formulate a 'model' of a central economy, as he calls it. In Amin's work the attributes of self-sustained growth are set out in the model of a 'self-centred system' (Amin, 1974c, which summarizes *L'accumulation à l'échelle mondiale* 1971; English translation, Amin, 1974a), further elaborated in his *Le développement inégal* (1973; English translation, Amin, 1976) in which a terminology of 'autocentric accumulation' and 'autocentric and autodynamic growth' is introduced. It is only the advanced capitalist countries that have truly *national* economies

each of which *alone* constitutes a true, structured economic space within which progress is diffused from industries that can be regarded as poles of development (1976, p. 238, emphasis added). This means that the advanced economy is an integrated whole, a feature of which is a very dense flow of internal exchanges, the flow of external exchanges of the atoms that make up this whole being, by and large, marginal as compared with that of internal exchanges (*ibid*, p. 237).

The effect of this formulation is to drive a wedge between the theorization of the advanced capitalist economies (as individual entities) and the theorization of world economy. To this extent it seems anomalous within underdevelopment theory which takes capitalist world economy as its field of study and source of explanations. On the other hand, it exemplifies the same conceptual dualism which constitutes world economy through 'models' of developed and underdeveloped countries, even if the former is latent in most expressions of underdevelopment theory.

The 'central determining relationship' in advanced capitalist economies is that between Marx's Department I and Department II (production of means of production and of means of consumption respectively). The proportionality between the Departments in relation to income distribution and effective demand is the crucial question of capitalism for Amin. The 'fundamental, permanent and growing contradiction (is) between the capacity to produce and the capacity to consume' (1976, p. 77, also pp. 92ff, 126, 173). At the same time this contradiction 'is continually being overcome through extending the market ever wider and deeper' (p. 92), which is made possible by the 'social contract' between labour and capital under the aegis of the state (since the Second World War), and by mechanisms of the absorption of excess capital. The 'social contract' regulating the relation of wages and productivity, and the means of 'surplus absorption' provided by the monopoly capitalist state, are the conditions permitting the continuous extended reproduction of capital in the central formations. Some of the effects of this process of adjustment, in particular the tendency of the rate of profit to fall, enter into and explain the relations between the central and peripheral formations, as does the widening of the market. However, these relations remain those of 'primitive accumulation' and are marginal to the process of extended reproduction within (each of) the advanced capitalist countries, which gives the content of their 'auto-centricity'.[12]

While this summary does not do justice to the complexity of Amin's argument, it illustrates the major points in relation to our present concerns. First, that the defining feature of advanced capitalist economies for underdevelopment theory is their 'self-sustaining', 'self-centred', 'autocentric', 'autodynamic' character. Second, these synonymous capacities, while little theorized (with the exception of Amin), provide a *'model of development'* through which the structures of underdeveloped or peripheral formations are conceptualized.

Underdevelopment: structure and process

The term 'underdevelopment' refers to these self-perpetuating processes, these self-reproducing structures, *and* to their results. The term 'dependency' is sometimes used to refer to exactly the same things, and sometimes more specifically to the non-autonomous nature of the laws and tendencies governing change in the social formations of the periphery. In spite of disagreements between the users of these two terms their differences seem less important than the extensive points of general agreement (Leys, 1977, p. 93).

What all agree on is the 'development of underdevelopment' as a historical process, as an intrinsic and necessary part of the capitalist world economy. The structure of the latter is formed by two kinds of economies, developed and underdeveloped or central and peripheral, constituted by their mutual relations which are unequal or asymmetrical. We have noted that the development of the advanced economies is characterized by self-sustained growth and the structural integration and proportionality of a 'self-centred' economic model.

The major issue concerning the structures of the peripheral formations has focused on the question of dualism, taking off from Frank's attack on the concept as presented both in bourgeois works (e.g. Furtado, 1964) and in the programmes of the Latin American Communist Parties (Frank, 1969a, especially Ch. 4). The latter proposed a class collaborationist strategy of alliance with a 'progressive' industrial or national bourgeoisie against the 'feudal oligarchy' of the agricultural sector in the interests of national (capitalist) development. Frank's position is that their incorporation into world capitalist economy through colonialism *ipso facto* converts pre-capitalist formations into capitalist formations of a 'satellite' type. The relationship with the 'metropole', expressed through production for the international market, is determinant and definitive of capitalism, overriding the forms of enterprises, modes of recruitment of labour and social organization of the labour processes through which that production takes place.[13]

In a notable criticism of this conception, Ernesto Laclau has outlined the concept of an 'economic system' which designates

the mutual relations between the different sectors of the economy, or between different productive units, whether on a regional, national or world scale . . . An economic system can include as constitutive elements, different modes of production—provided always that we define it as a whole, that is, by proceeding from the element or law of motion that establishes the unity of its different manifestations (1971, p. 33).

This idea has been elaborated further in the concept of the 'articulation of modes of production' by a number of French writers in particular (Bettelheim in Emmanuel, 1972; Rey, 1973, 1976; Godelier, 1974; Meillassoux, 1975).

The issue is one that continues to exercise underdevelopment theory, and revolves around the problem of characterizing social formations in which capitalism is dominant (in some sense) but in which neither capitalist production enterprises nor the commodity form of labour-power are generalized. The tension arising from this (genuine) problem is manifested in a range of formulations that have failed to solve it.

In a single text (1976), Samir Amin employs at least three different conceptualizations of the peripheral social formations. One coincides exactly with dualism of the bourgeois type attacked by Frank: the coexistence of separate sectors, often expressed as an export enclave and a subsistence sector. 'Two sectors coexist without interpenetrating and the economy does not form an integral unity' (p. 271). The second conforms to the idea of articulation of modes of production—'(In the peripheral formations) the capitalist mode, which is dominant, subjects the others and transforms them, depriving them of their distinctive functioning in order to subordinate them to its own, without, however, radically destroying them' (p. 22). Finally, 'Despite their different origins, the peripheral formations tend to converge toward a pattern that is essentially the same. This phenomenon reflects, on the world scale, the increasing power of capitalism to unify' (p. 333).

Another manifestation of this general problem is the proliferation of modes of production in the recent literature. Hamza Alavi, for example, has formulated the concept of a 'colonial mode of production' precisely to avoid treating the Indian colonial formation as an articulated combination of capitalist and feudal modes. The colonial mode 'is a (sic) capitalist mode of production' (1975, p. 191) but a 'deformed' one. It exhibits 'a colonial form of deformed generalized commodity production' and 'a (colonial form of) deformed extended reproduction'. The first arises from the disarticulation of the colonial economy (a concept taken from Amin), the elements of which 'were no longer integrated internally and directly but only by virtue of the separate ties of its different segments with the metropolitan economy'. The second feature is the (surplus drain) effect of the first: 'The result of the internal disarticulation of the colonial economy and the extraction of the surplus by the colonial power meant that the extended reproduction could not be realized within the economy of the colony but could be realized only through the imperialist centre' (ibid, p. 187).[14]

Other writers have suggested the emergence of new modes of production under colonialism. For example, Pierre-Philippe Rey designates the forms of exploitation of their followers established by the marabouts in colonial Senegal a mode of production which is non-capitalist but dominated by capitalism (1976, p. 63). As a final illustration, a 'peasant mode of production' appears at various points in the work of Amin. 'The peasant goes on producing within the setting of his former mode of production, but henceforth he produces commodities that are exported to the centre' (1976, p. 294, In another work on the agrarian question, he characterizes the 'peasant mode of production' as one of the family of simple commodity modes—Amin, 1974b).[15] The indeterminacy of the concept of mode of production by the time it has undergone these mutations is such that it is not surprising to find an anthropologist employing the concept of articulation, together with that of 'structural dependency', and compiling a list of 'modes of production' encountered in his field-work area (Long, 1975, 1977).[16]

Given these examples of the difficulties experienced in formulating the structure of the peripheral formations, it may be suggested that this is an impossible task at a general level but one forced on underdevelopment theory by its posing of 'underdevelopment' as a unitary object of investigation. In this respect, Amin's 'convergence thesis' noted above is illustrative. It prefaces a section on 'The General Characteristics of the Peripheral Formations' (1976, pp. 333–364).

All peripheral formations have four main characteristics in common: (1) the predominance of agrarian capitalism in the national sector; (2) the creation of a local, mainly merchant, bourgeoisie in the wake of foreign capital; (3) a tendency toward a peculiar bureaucratic development, specific to the contemporary periphery; (4) the incomplete, specific character of the phenomena of proletarianization (emphasis added).

From these formulations and the discussion that follows it is evident that these 'general characteristics' are not theoretically specified, but are empirical generalizations (and of a low order). Most of the examples are drawn from Africa, and the generalizations themselves are subject to subclassifications that are crudely inductivist in form—for example, different 'model(s) for the constitution of a national bourgeoisie' for Europe, 'the Eastern world', and 'contemporary Black Africa' (p. 339).[17]

This attempt to generalize the structure of underdevelopment (as with Amin's 'model' of an autocentric economic system) is useful as it makes explicit an effect of the mode of conceptualization of underdevelopment theory that remains implicit, but nonetheless real, in other texts. This is an effect of the very act of constituting 'underdevelopment' as a unitary object of investigation. It is because the 'development of underdevelopment' is posed as a unitary process, as the necessary consequence of a particular structural position in world economy, that underdevelopment theory is compelled towards a unitary conception of the structure of underdeveloped formations. This effect is hidden behind the discussion of different 'forms' of underdevelopment, either in historical sequence or as contemporary variants, but insofar as these are 'phenomenal' forms (empirically described) of an 'essential' process, this conception can only yield a linear history of the underdevelopment of the periphery as a whole or of particular formations within it.[18]

The content of this history is always the domination of the periphery by the centre, the exploitation of the former (surplus drain), and the reproduction of underdevelopment. At best it is a history of successive 'forms' but only as the changing expressions of a basic continuity.

(There is) a third contradiction in capitalist economic development and underdevelopment: The *continuity* and ubiquity of economic development and underdevelopment throughout the expansion and development of the capitalist system *at all times and places* (Frank, 1969a, p. 12, emphases added).

At every stage in the development of the world capitalist system the commercial and financial relations between the center and periphery thus serve *the same twofold function*: on one hand, to facilitate, by extending the capitalist market at the expense of the precapitalist systems, the absorption of the surplus, and, on the other, to increase the average rate of profit (Amin, 1976a, pp. 187–8, emphases added).

G.

The 'classic' structure of underdevelopment is associated with the occupa-
tion of a particular place in the international division of labour, and en-
capsulates the features of an 'export economy' producing agricultural and
mineral raw materials for the industries of the centre (a characterization
that underdevelopment shares with some bourgeois works, *inter alia*,
Myint, 1958; Levin, 1960; Furtado, 1964). In this conception, then, one
of the attributes of underdevelopment is the lack of industry other than
that required for the production and transporting of raw materials. The
post-war development of manufacturing industry in some parts of the
Third World has been accommodated by a revision of the attributes of
underdevelopment so that they can now include industrialization but of a
necessarily limited or 'dependent' kind.

Significantly, the notion of 'dependence' emerged in Latin American
debates concerning the experience of *desarrollo hacia adentro* or 'inner-
directed' development through import-substituting industrialization advo-
cated by the nationalist economists of the Economic Commission for Latin
America in the 1950s, in opposition to *desarrollo hacia afuera*, the 'out-
ward-directed' promotion of exports favoured by conventional growth
models. The effects of import-substitution, including the pressures on
foreign exchange required for importing capital goods (and the indebted-
ness and inflation associated with this), and the opportunities it gave to
multinational corporations to establish manufacturing subsidiaries or to
exploit their advantages in technology in other ways, produced a disillusionment with *desarrollo hacia adentro* (Dos Santos, 1973; Booth, 1975;
O'Brien, 1975). This disillusionment was expressed as the failure of 'inner-
directed' development *in its own terms*, that is, as the strategy of a truly
national and 'autonomous' capitalist development, and it is this which
gives the term 'dependence' its ideological poignancy.

The concept of dependence widened the scope of underdevelopment
theory insofar as it freed it from its stagnationist associations, which
in the 'export economy model' limited growth to the increased production
of export commodities without any effect on the development of production
for the internal market (Cardoso, 1972). 'Dependency theory' therefore
allows growth (including the expansion of the domestic market) to be
accommodated with underdevelopment but without changing the 'essential'
structures of the latter.

Control or lack of control over technology is now seen as a central
factor, intensifying the grip of international capital already established
by its financial power (Frank, 1969a, Ch. 5; Dos Santos, 1973; Alavi,
1975; Amin, 1976). For Alavi the colonial mode may be superseded by a
'post-colonial' mode of production in which the circuits of generalized
commodity production, and the extended reproduction of capital, are
realized internally (at least in part) but 'external dependence' is manifested 'in the field of capital goods and research intensive technology'
(1975, p. 192). Amin talks of a transition 'from specialization to dependence'
(1976, Ch. 3): 'the investment of physical capital loses its importance as a
means of obtaining extra surplus-value in order to increase the monopolies'
rate of profit. Technological domination is increasingly adequate to
accomplish this task' (*ibid*, p. 189).[19]

Modifications of the process of 'development of underdevelopment' are
reflected in changes in terminology—thus 'neoimperialism' (Frank, Amin)
and 'postimperialism' (Amin again), but this expansion of the vocabulary

of underdevelopment theory does not signify any development of its theoretical apparatus. The proliferation of neologisms only consolidates the same basic tenets—*plus ça change, plus c'est la même chose* as Booth has noted in a discussion of the work of Frank (1975, p. 77). Likewise Amin for whom 'dependent' industrialization is only the latest form of an unequal international specialization that always constitutes a mechanism of primitive accumulation to the advantage of the center' (1976, p. 190). The forms of 'advanced' underdevelopment including manufacturing industry (even of capital goods) only disarticulate the peripheral economies further and intensify their underdevelopment. There are no qualitative (theoretically specified) differences between the development of capitalism in formations like those of Brazil and India and those like Senegal, the structures of these formations exhibiting only a quantitative difference in the numbers of their links to the centres of world capitalism (*ibid*, p. 238).

The impossibility of a theory of underdevelopment

Following the above review it is now possible to argue both that a theory of underdevelopment is impossible, and that attempts to construct such a theory are ideologically determined. This involves a further consideration of the concept of 'development' which informs all the formulations of underdevelopment in much the same way that the models of modernity determine the sociological theories of modernization. There is a double aspect of the pervasive, if often lurking, notion of 'development'. On one hand, it denotes that capitalist development has been achieved in the centre but cannot be repeated in the periphery; on the other hand it betrays a utopian conception of development.

To the extent that the development of the centre is realized through the underdevelopment of the periphery, and that these are fixed positions, then by definition the periphery cannot develop within the existing relations of the world system. However, as we have noted, there is a pervasive image (it cannot be termed anything else as long as it remains implicit and untheorized) of 'development' as involving self-sustained growth based on an integrated and self-centred economic structure. This has been made explicit, exceptionally, by Samir Amin, but the result of constituting a model of self-centred economy is to undermine the effectivity of world economy and its mechanisms.

That world economy is as much a condition of existence of advanced capitalist economies as of underdeveloped ones; that the bulk of international capital flows and trade takes place between the advanced capitalist countries; that production for the international market has been important throughout the history of industrial capitalism; that the internationalization of productive capital, the interpenetration of capitals, and the internationalization of production processes they increasingly entail, are of central importance to the advanced capitalist economies; that, in short, they are no more 'autonomous' than the underdeveloped economies —all this is lost at the moment of making self-centredness the distinguishing attribute of 'development'. One writer, drawing on Samir Amin, has pursued the idea of the national 'self-reliance' of advanced capitalism to its absurd conclusion: the exports of the developed countries 'are incidental to production for the domestic market and in general only the spill-over is exported'! (Tschannerl, 1976, p. 14).[20]

(The) economic development that does occur in the more prosperous of the
satellites is at best a limited or 'underdeveloped' development. It is constantly
conditioned by relationships of dependence upon the metropolis. Economic
development in Latin America, in other words, is a satellite development, which
is *not autonomous to the region, self-generating or self-perpetuating* (Cockcroft,
Frank and Johnson, 1972, p. xi, emphasis added).

Underdevelopment theory cannot have it both ways. If the field of analysis
is world economy, if the centre needs the periphery for modes of exploitation that off-set the tendency of the rate of profit to fall, if the circuit of
capital in general is realized on the international plane, then there is *no*
capitalist formation whose development can be regionally autonomous,
self-generating or self-perpetuating. 'Development' cannot be conceptualized by its self-centred nature and lack of dependence, nor 'underdevelopment' by its dependence and lack of autonomy.

Just as the process of modernization is legislated by the models of
sociology and political science, the notion of a 'normal' capitalist development, realized in the centre but denied the periphery, encourages the
conceptualization of the latter in terms of shortfall from the norm. Whatever changes occur, being responses to impulses from the centre (Frank,
1972b, p. 39; Magdoff, 1972, p. 146; Amin, 1976, p. 345), are not 'developmental' but express an 'ongoing *mis*development' (Cockcroft, Frank
and Johnson, 1972, p. xviii). In Alavi's colonial mode of production
generalized commodity production and accumulation are *deformed*; in
Amin's peripheral formations and Beckford's plantation economy model
(1969, 1972) resource allocation is *distorted*.

In these symptomatic examples, the character of capitalist underdevelopment is established as problematic only by reference to a 'model' of
capitalist development that is non-problematic. In a similar way the debate
on the post-colonial state has posed the question of identifying the ruling-
class and its component fractions. The question is defined as one specific
to the formations of the Third World in contrast to the advanced capitalist
countries where the 'classic' equation: economically dominant class =
ruling class, holds good and the state is therefore non-problematic (Alavi,
1972; Shivji, 1975).[21]

The concept of 'development' employed by the radical theorists, in
addition to its derivation from a notion of 'normal' capitalist development,
incorporates elements from the welfarism of 'left-liberal' development
studies and from nationalist ideology. The former, expressed classically
by Seers and reprinted here, is the charter of the social-democratic stream
of the development studies profession: 'the meaning of development' is not
exhausted by the need to promote economic growth but must include a
more egalitarian distribution of its fruits, the guarantee of basic human
and civil rights, equality of opportunity, and so on. The extent to which
this 'meaning of development' has been absorbed by radical underdevelopment theory is expressed characteristically in *moral* critiques of
capitalism (or at least capitalist underdevelopment), and in the vocabulary
of social inequality and unequal development.

'Increasing social inequality is the mode of reproduction of the conditions of externally oriented development' (Amin, 1976, p. 352), Alavi,
commenting on the effects of the Green Revolution in India, states: 'It
has greatly intensified the inequalities. We are witness to a strange paradox

—a pattern of development that has not only created much wealth for a few but simultaneously and necessarily, greater poverty for the many' (1975, p. 167). Why is this a paradox in a capitalist social formation? Certainly Marx and Lenin would not have regarded it as such, but rather as one of the conditions of the formation of agrarian capital.[22]

The second element, that of nationalist ideology, has already been indicated in our discussion of the emergence of the concept of dependence as an expression of disillusionment with the strategy of 'inner-directed' development *in its own terms*, that is, bemoaning the failure of the industrial bourgeoisie of Latin America to meet the challenge of becoming a truly *national* bourgeoisie. As Phillips has commented—'National capital has been given the opportunity to put itself forward as representing the "national interest", and has been ultimately rejected not because it is *capital,* but because it is unable to be sufficiently *national'* (1977, p. 19). This judgement, as she further notes, is linked to an uncritical assimilation of the concept of 'national development' by radical underdevelopment theory.

Theory has been defined as 'a logical structure of concepts which designates an object to be explained and which provides a mechanism of explanation for that object' (Hirst, 1976, p. 78). A theory of underdevelopment is impossible because 'underdevelopment' does not constitute a coherent object of explanation. As we saw with modernization theories, a non-problematic model of modernity provides the conceptual means by which both non-modernity is defined and the process of modernization is legislated. The dualism established by the conceptual couple, modernity-tradition, embodies a circularity which cannot produce any theoretical advance, any explanation other than that already given by definition of the terms. Concrete analysis consists of the accretion of facts around these terms and their derivatives.

The same is true of underdevelopment theory. Underdevelopment is constituted as the negative expression of 'development'. On one hand development is associated with a 'model' of 'normal' (or 'classic') capitalist development, combining an integrated national economy and autocentric accumulation as the basis of self-sustained growth, which is simultaneously rendered impossible by the postulate that the capitalist development of the centre has as its necessary condition the underdevelopment of the periphery. This is an effect of the lack of an adequate theorization and *problematization* of the concept of capitalism. Modernization theory ultimately assures the goal of modernity or development as long as the correct prescriptions are followed; underdevelopment theory asserts that whatever changes occur in the peripheral formations they will never achieve development within the capitalist world system. Despite substantial industrialization, despite the expansion of the domestic market, they cannot become autonomous or non-dependent—but then no capitalist formation can be. Or, it signifies that no formation in the Third World can become another United States, which is a negative teleology: stating what cannot occur provides no means of investigating what does occur.[23]

The other notion of 'development' which informs the conceptualization of underdevelopment is a utopian construct: development as the realization of the creative energies of 'the people' mobilized for the good of the nation. The utopian conception describes what is ('underdevelopment')

through a vision of what ought to be ('development') which provides a
moralistic critique of capitalism. It is not only that moralism fails to provide the means for investigating capitalism and explaining it but that it
actively undermines this task.

The way in which underdevelopment is constituted as an object of theory
replicates the circularity of the modernization models, and is likewise
expressed in a series of conceptual polarities: developed/underdeveloped,
metropole/satellite, centre/periphery, autocentric growth/extraverted
growth, domination/dependence. Underdevelopment is posed as a unitary
process with uniform causes and uniform effects, which is why underdevelopment theory is unable to produce a differentiated history of
capital. The essential continuity suggested yields a linear history of the
reproduction of underdevelopment, established through a 'verificationist'
accumulation of the facts of exploitation and oppression. Social change can
only be accommodated by a proliferating and derivative vocabulary and
not by any development of concepts and means of explanation—thus
advanced underdevelopment, ultraunderdevelopment, unequal development, lumpendevelopment, dependent development, dependent bourgeoisie, lumpenbourgeoisie, comprador bourgeoisie, semi-colonial, neo-
colonial, post-colonial, neoimperialism, sub-imperialism, sub-metropole,
semi-periphery . . . and so on.

Marxism, Sociology and Development

Is radical underdevelopment theory Marxist? The answer must be
negative. Through the mystifying use of a Marxist terminology—capitalism, imperialism, accumulation, class struggle—are expressed concepts
which are derived from other problematics. Some of these have been
indicated: a structuralist and underconsumptionist political economy, in
which the social relations of production and their variant conditions and
forms cannot be posed as problematic, in which 'contradiction' and 'exploitation' are metaphorical rather than analytical terms, in which a static
notion of capital operates innocent of the complex and differentiated
structure of concepts and their relations by which the theory of *Capital* is
constituted[24]; the use of a 'model' of 'normal' capitalist development which
is contrary to Marxism and appropriates some of its categories by the
methods of bourgeois social science in ways that necessarily, if subtly,
change their content; the use of a moralistic and idealist critique of
capitalism based on philosophical humanism, which condemns the
objective effects of the contradictory nature of capitalist development by
reference to a utopia free of exploitation, oppression and dependence.[25]

The result ultimately is that underdevelopment theory, despite its
vigorous ideological offensive against the models of conventional development studies, *fails to achieve a theoretical break with them.* As Colin Leys
has expressed it in a brilliant metaphor—'the "marxification" of radical
structuralism, or "left" UDT (underdevelopment theory) does not rescue
radical structuralism from its dilemma, for the basic reason that it has
been built up through successive revisions of bourgeois social science,
especially bourgeois economics, and like a Russian doll, the final outer
layer has essentially the same shape as the innermost one' (1977, p. 98).

Where does 'neo-Marxism' come in? Foster-Carter acknowledges that
radical underdevelopment theory originates as an ideological critique of

bourgeois development models. It then develops further in opposition to 'traditional Marxism' (1974, p. 84ff). In contrast to the latter, it is 'open-minded . . . viewing the world inductively', it is interested in imperialism from the viewpoint of its victims (compare 'Dependence is imperialism seen from the perspective of underdevelopment', Johnson, 1972a, p. 71), which is a 'shift of emphasis (that) of course parallels the emergence of the Third World as an actor in its own right'. This is followed by an inventory of themes which neo-Marxism treats differently from its dogmatic ancestor: nationalism, classes, revolution, communism, morals and action, town and country, and ecology. The type of politics suggested by neo-Marxist sociology is something we shall return to shortly.[26]

At this point the question may be asked in some bewilderment—where is *sociology* in all this? One right-wing critic, in the course of bemoaning 'the flight of culture among students of development', attacks 'the current orthodoxy' (radical underdevelopment theory) and its effects. 'Values, culture, behavioural dispositions are out. The reading lists of Sociology of Development courses in this country (Britain) are dominated by amateur economics' (Dore, 1976, p. 2). Radical underdevelopment theory is not a rigorous political economy, as we have argued, but neither, *contra* Professor Dore, is it incompatible with sociological discourse. Its mode of theorization precisely lends itself to the sociologization of Marxist concepts.

The work of Immanuel Wallerstein provides a very clear example of this process. The substantive propositions of underdevelopment theory (expressed as centre/periphery relations) are brought into the service of a comparative sociology of world empires and world economy (1974a, Ch. 7, 1974b). Empires and economies are 'systems' constituted by the mutually conditioning behaviour of 'actors'—variously states, 'classes' and individuals. Because Wallerstein's world system is 'capitalist', busily developing core areas and underdeveloping peripheral ones, the first volume of his history was welcomed with extravagant praise by Gunder Frank. Wallerstein's total lack of comprehension of Marxist categories is exemplified in his criticism of Laclau (1971). 'Capitalism . . . means labour (*sic*) as a commodity to be sure . . . (but) how could labour-power be ever more a commodity than under slavery?' (1974b, p. 400). One might ask by extension, how then could 'capitalism' ever be more developed than it was in the plantation colonies of the seventeenth and eighteenth-century Caribbean?[27]

What is more serious politically for Marxism is the sociologization of the categories and method of class analysis. Foster-Carter in approving the neo-Marxist focus on imperialism 'as it presents itself to its victims, how it attacks them, and how it can be defeated', in the next sentence goes on to speak of 'the emergence of the Third World as an actor in its own right' (1974, p. 85). We are thus presented with 'class struggle' between two 'actors': imperialism (the oppressor) and 'the Third World' (the victim). His discussion lays bare the consequent assimilation of class struggle to the perspective of a subjectivist sociology—'Marxism needs its own phenomenology' (*ibid*, p. 92). 'Liberation' is subsumed in a phenomenological explosion of 'consciousness':

Marxism has become a world-view whereby hitherto inchoate or subdued groups take hold of their reality and, in Mao's simple but graphic phrase, 'stand up' to assert themselves. From this angle, such apparently diverse phenomena as Black Power, student power, women's liberation, gay liberation ('out of the toilets and into the streets'), *and* peasant revolutionary nationalism in colonial countries, are all part of a single trend (*ibid*, p. 87).

This statement is no doubt an unusually flamboyant expression of the syndrome, but the reduction of class analysis to the sociological problematic of inequality, of privilege and deprivation, is a widespread effect of underdevelopment theory.

Viewed internally, the key point about Latin America's class structure is its polarization into those classes with jobs, income, status and participation in society as against those classes either without employment or in jobs of high exploitation. Among the classes that together form a 'marginal mass' are most Indians, peasants, unemployed or underemployed workers, and highly exploited service workers. On the other end of the scale are the best paid of the stable working class, the entrenched middle class, and the dominant bourgeoisie of urban elites and landholders (Cockcroft, Frank and Johnson, 1972, p. xvi).[28]

Both Leys (1977) and Phillips (1977) have noted that class analysis has entered underdevelopment theory by default. The historic incapacity of the comprador or dependent bourgeoisies to carry through the 'national development' postulated by an idealist conception (taken over from the ideological enemy) has pushed underdevelopment theory to seek other agents of development. Revolution and socialism are now on the agenda as an effect of the failure of national capitalist development. 'The people' (and their leaders) are seen as the collective subject of 'real development', a form of populism which, while it may employ the language of class analysis and call on the slogans of class struggle, lacks the weapon of revolutionary theory which is necessary to any effective socialist politics.[29]

The immediate effect of 'marxifying' radical structuralism was to shift the implied solution to the problem of underdevelopment from economic nationalism to *socialism*, and to shift the means from utopian recommendations of radical structural reforms to *revolutionary struggle*. But this is an illusion. It is no less utopian to appeal to 'revolution' and 'socialism' to solve the problem as *radical structuralism formulates it*, than to the existing third world governments or the USAID, since a structuralist analysis doesn't disclose the potential class forces or organisational forms of struggle, or—*a fortiori*—a 'socialist' solution, since a socialist solution must itself be disclosed by the interests and capacities of the revolutionary forces and their strategy which have not been identified at all (Leys, 1977, p. 98).

CONCLUSION

The *wishes* of the romanticists are very good (as are those of the Narodniks). Their recognition of the contradictions of capitalism places them above the blind optimists who deny the existence of these contradictions (Lenin, 1960 IIa, p. 242).

The radical sociology of underdevelopment recognizes the contradictions of capitalism and it has demolished the modernization models, the blind optimism of which turns to moral censure as soon as their prescriptions are ignored. In the course of its career, radical underdevelopment theory has certainly elaborated in useful ways the 'symptomology' of the uneven development of capitalism on the world scale. The good wishes of the underdevelopment theorists (that is, their subjective commitment) are not in question, but then it is not a question of great importance.[30] What is of great importance is the objective struggle of ideas. The Narodniks' recognition of capitalist contradictions from a moralist position meant that they were unable to produce an objective analysis of the process of capitalist development in Russia.[31]

On one side there is historical materialism, on the other there is the variety of theoretical and ideological currents in bourgeois philosophy and social sciences. The blurring of the incompatibility and antagonism between the two through the medium of a radical sociology of underdevelopment, or any other radicalization of social science, can only result in the subversion of Marxism to the benefit of the bourgeois order. The failure of underdevelopment theory to effect a theoretical break with bourgeois social science soon undermines the initial gains from its ideological offensive. A process of 'conservative re-absorption' begins (Kay, 1975, Introduction; Leys, 1977), of which one example should be sufficient.

The change of emphasis brought about by neo-Marxism was necessary and overdue ... Robert McNamara's speeches (following the one that he made to UNCTAD III in 1972) have suddenly focused on the needs of the neglected poor. The first step has therefore been taken, and income distribution has become a live issue (de Kadt, 1974, pp. 3, 14).

The juxtaposition of these two statements suggests a connection that their author may or may not have intended, but the relationship is not merely fanciful. The ideological flexibility of which practical bourgeois thought is capable, particularly as articulated by those institutions like the World Bank which have a crucial ideological role, serves as a warning to the radical sociologists. The only theory able to inform the struggles of the proletariat and other exploited classes throughout the world is that of historical materialism, which is itself the site of a continuous struggle to maintain its integrity and hence its effectiveness.

NOTES

1. This has led to the charge of ethnocentrism being levelled against the sociology of development, e.g. by Abdel-Malek, 1967.

2. Thus McClelland in an article first published in the *Harvard Business Review* 'Unless we learn our lesson and find ways of stimulating that drive for achievement under freedom in poor countries, the Communists will go on providing it all around the world. We can go on building dikes to maintain freedom and impoverishing ourselves to feed and arm the people behind those dikes, but only if we develop the entrepreneurial spirit in these countries will we have a sound foreign policy. Only then can they look after their own dikes and become economically self-sufficient' (McClelland, 1964, p. 176).

3. The affinity between evolutionism and a certain conception of 'Comparative Method' is not accidental—see Nisbet, 1969, Ch. 6. In the political science literature 'political development', 'political modernization' and 'comparative politics' serve as interchangeable terms for that branch of the discipline concerned with the countries of the Third World.

4. The residual conception of the 'non-economic' reflects both the division of labour in the bourgeois social sciences and the dominance of *Economics* in that division of labour—a dominance appropriate to the character of capitalist society.

5. 'The dual economy model comprises a theory of underdevelopment premised on the coexistence within a given national economy of two more or less autonomous

sectors, a modern sector and a backward or traditional sector. The modernity of the former (typically a veiled synonym for capitalist economic aims, methods, and social relations) centres on industry, urban services, and/or the production of export commodities in large units such as plantations. The backward sector consists of peasant agriculture with a large subsistence component, a low level of technological development, under-utilisation of labour, and archaic social organisation. In dualist theory it is this sector which exhibits the characteristics of the "low-level equilibrium trap", which inhibits the formation of sufficient internal demand to stimulate the "take-off" of national industry, which reproduces "traditional" value-orientations and behaviour—in sum, which presents a series of "obstacles" to development, the impetus to which is created in the modern sector' (Bernstein and Pitt, 1974, p. 516).

6. This statement by Lerner resonates a disillusionment with the 'revolution of rising expectations' previously celebrated as the motivational engine of development and modernization. The expectations of the masses of the poor and oppressed once aroused, however, are not easily satisfied in the conditions of capitalism. Lerner's response is to detect an alarming gap between the subjective aspiration to the good life and the objective need to work for it—the laziness of the 'natives' rediscovered. How this bears on 'the problem of order' is clearly expressed by Ithiel da Sola Pool, a prominent 'new mandarin' of the Vietnam period quoted by Chomsky (1969, p. 33)

'In the Congo, in Vietnam, in the Dominican Republic, it is clear that order depends on somehow compelling newly mobilized strata to return to a measure of passivity and defeatism from which they have been aroused by the process of modernization. At least temporarily, the maintenance of order requires a lowering of newly acquired aspirations and levels of political activity.'

7. 'And we will help you . . .' by the provision of aid, technical assistance, transfer of technology etc., the diffusionist rationale of which is indicated in the passage from Eisenstadt quoted above. For a discussion of diffusionism see Frank, 1967.

8. The radicals are hardly alone in pointing this out. The failure to close the 'development gap' and the continuing (or worsening) plight of the poor are standard themes of the 'left-wing' of the development studies profession and in recent years of the World Bank itself. This is reflected in the focus on employment and income distribution that has emerged in the 1970s.

9. See note 6 above; also Cruise O'Brien, 1972, reprinted in this volume.

10. The concept of a 'problematic' employed in this passage (and throughout this essay) derives from recent debates in Marxist theory stimulated by the work of Louis Althusser, and more particularly from joint work with Jacques Depelchin and others at the University of Dar es Salaam on theory and method in African history (Bernstein and Depelchin, 1978).

11. Among useful discussions critical of particular underdevelopment or dependency theories from a Marxist position are those by Arrighi, 1971; Laclau, 1971; Taylor, 1974; Booth, 1975; O'Brien, 1975; Gerstein, 1977; critical discussions from a bourgeois position include those by Nove, 1974, and Hopkins, 1975. The incisive articles by Leys, 1977, and Phillips, 1977, argue more generally that a theory of underdevelopment is impossible and that attempts to construct such a theory are ideologically determined, which is the conclusion of this essay. It is appropriate at this point to express my thanks for a number of stimulating discussions to Gary Littlejohn and Harold Wolpe whom I was fortunate to have as neighbours in Dar es Salaam at different stages of this work. I also benefited from a preliminary testing of its arguments against the formidable dialectical skills of Michaela von Freyhold even if I failed to convince her completely. Mahmood Mamdani has pointed out a number of issues *not* covered here but within the scope of one essay it is impossible to respond to every issue raised by underdevelopment theory which, after all, proposes the framework of a history of capitalism over four centuries. The purpose here is modest—by indicating the errors of underdevelopment theory to clear the way for a more scientific understanding of the basis of such a project (see note 24 below).

12. The work of Samir Amin is particularly important for current underdevelopment theory because of its scope, its awareness of problems ignored by others employing this approach (e.g. Frank), and its claim to be Marxist without qualification. On the other hand, Amin's major texts (1974a, 1976; I have not had the opportunity to read his 1976a) contain an encyclopaedic tangle of categories and method which is self-reinforcing and results in a series of mutually contradictory propositions, so that it is a lengthy task to untie all the knots and unravel the strands of which they are composed. I hope to provide such a guide to reading Amin in an extended review of his *Unequal Development*.

For the moment several comments can be made. The first concerns Amin's difficulties with the concepts of mode of production and social formation, and in particular the relation between the categories of the capitalist mode of production and their application to the analysis of capitalist social formations (central and peripheral, in his terms) and the relations between them (world economy). For example, compare the following (all from his 1976):

'By way of exception among social formations, the central capitalist social formation tends to become identical with the mode of production that dominates it' (p. 77), and 'there is no question that any socio-economic formation of capitalism at the centre can be reduced to a pure capitalist mode of production' (p. 139); 'what is involved (in centre-periphery relations, H.B.) is not the mechanisms characteristic of the internal functioning of the capitalist mode of production but relations between this mode of production and formations that are different from it' (p. 147), and 'the phenomena of marginalization (in the periphery, H.B.) are nothing more than the expression of the fundamental laws of the capitalist mode of production under the concrete conditions of the world capitalist system' (p. 363).

Second, in the model of the central economy, Amin's concepts of the 'social contract' between labour and capital and of 'surplus absorption' draw on the work of Emmanuel (1972) and Baran and Sweezy (1966) respectively, which share a basic theoretical under-consumptionism. Emmanuel regards international wage differentials as the source of unequal exchange, wages being the 'independent variable' in the determination of prices of commodities in the world market. Wages themselves are determined by an institutional process of bargaining between labour and capital 'exogenous' to the market process through which the prices of other 'factors of production' are formed. The impossibility of constituting wages as an 'independent variable', the conflation of value and price of labour-power, of the use-value and value of commodities, and of exchange of non-equivalent values and exchange of unequal amounts of labour, have been pointed out by Emmanuel's critics (Bettelheim in his Appendices to Emmanuel, 1972; Pilling, 1973; Kay, 1975, pp. 107–119; Mandel, 1975, pp. 351–64). Emmanuel ties development to the sequence: high wages→effective demand→growth of the domestic market→expansion of production. This yields a 'model' of *under*development which replicates exactly the 'vicious circle' theory of Nurkse (1953), although the assertion of *low* wages as the 'independent variable' does alter what is otherwise an undetermined circularity. Amin, while critical of some aspects of Emmanuel's formulation of unequal exchange (Amin, 1973) follows it in its main lines as a 'fundamental contribution' (1976, p. 138ff.).

Amin's relationship to the economics of the '*Monthly Review* school' is also significant. As various commentators have noted, Baran's *The Political Economy of Growth* (1957) was a pioneering work from which contemporary underdevelopment theory draws much of its inspiration. In this text Baran presents the concept of 'economic surplus' (Ch. 2) which is central to the subsequent joint work on *Monopoly Capital* with Sweezy (1966) from which Amin draws the idea of surplus absorption. An exceptionally clear critique of the concept of economic surplus and its place in the theory of Baran and Sweezy is presented in Culley (1977).

Third, the position that in Amin's work a Marxist vocabulary serves as the medium through which a structuralist (that is, non-Marxist) conception of capitalism operates has been well argued by Wuyts, 1976 (see also R. Banaji, 1976; Disney, 1977, in a review of Amin, 1974a). Both Wuyts and Disney make the point that the effect of this structuralism is necessarily economistic despite Amin's emphatic strictures against economism. (Leys, 1977, indicates the relationship of 'marxified structuralism' and economism in his more general review of underdevelopment theory). Amin's references to class struggle are theoretically gratuitous in the sense that class struggle is not intrinsic to his analysis but is imposed on it in an ideological fashion. Similarly, the coherence and appeal of his texts, to the extent that they are ideological, can only be the product of an ideological reading.

As a final point in an inordinately long footnote, it should be made clear that it is not Samir Amin (or any other underdevelopment theorist) who is being criticised, but the character and effects of certain positions contained in his (or their) texts. This needs to be said given the *ad hominem* manner in which Amin himself tends to answer his critics, and also in view of changes in his position as illustrated in a recent article (1977)—see note 20 below.

13. And the various components of the 'lumpenbourgeoisie'—agrarian, commercial, industrial—form a bloc with a united interest in the reproduction of underdevelopment.

14. Although elaborated in the context of an Indian debate Alavi's concepts of colonial and post-colonial modes of production are intended to have a wider application (1975, p. 193). The concept of a colonial mode of production has also been put forward by Banaji (1972) who subsequently rejected it without, however, dismissing the questions to which the concept was a proposed solution. Banaji, 1975b, provides a critique of Alavi's formulation. The theorization of a colonial mode of production by von Freyhold (n.d.) stems from independent investigation in Tanzanian history and arrives at a position much closer to that of Pierre-Philippe Rey.

15. On the concept of peasant economy, mode of production etc. see Ennew, Hirst and Tribe, 1977. This concept received its most rigorous formulation in the work of A. V. Chayanov (Thorner, Kerblay and Smith ed., 1966) which is the object of a thorough critique by Littlejohn, 1977.

16. The availability of the definitive Marxist concept of mode of production to appropriation and descriptive use by non-Marxists has been facilitated by its presentation in texts like that of Terray (1972) which tends to reduce the concept of mode of production to different forms of the labour process. For a critical consideration of its use by Rey, see Tribe (1976), and on this issue more generally the incisive and important paper by Banaji (1975a).

17. The experience of reading much of the underdevelopment literature alerts one to the possibility that the appearance of the terms 'essence', 'essential' or 'essentially' announces an attempt to plug a theoretical gap. In this case, Amin's description of the structure of peripheral formations as 'essentially the same', the theoretical elision is effected by empirical generalizations.

18. Critics have made this point in relation to Frank's histories of Chile and Brazil (1969a, Chs. 1 and 3). The best-known radical history of African underdevelopment is that by Rodney (1972); the work of the Hungarian writer Endre Sik on Africa (1966, 1974) also exemplifies the features of this mode of historical writing (see Bernstein, 1977).

19. Technology has recently been taken up in a very similar way, that is, in its associations with multinational corporations, 'dependence' and dualism, by liberal development economists—see the special issue of the *Journal of Development Studies*, 1972, on 'Science and Technology in Development', especially the Introduction by C. Cooper; also Singer and Ansari, 1977. It seems that the only feature that is left to distinguish Alavi's post-colonial mode from the capitalist mode of production is an industrial bourgeoisie that is 'dependent' by virtue of its imports of advanced technology.

20. Samir Amin's 'model' establishes extended reproduction as the concept of autocentric accumulation in the central economies, and 'primitive accumulation' as the concept of 'surplus transfer' in centre-periphery relations. The purpose of this distinction is both to modify the necessity of 'surplus transfer' as a condition of sustained growth at the centre and to avoid the kind of 'automatic collapse' view of capitalism associated with the underconsumptionist theory of Rosa Luxemburg:

Between the production of surplus value, then, and the subsequent period of accumulation, two separate transactions take place—that of realizing the surplus value, i.e. of converting it into pure value, and that of transforming this pure value into productive capital. They are both dealings between capitalist production and the surrounding non-capitalist world. From the aspect both of realizing the surplus value and of procuring the material elements of constant capital, international trade is a prime necessity for the historical existence of capitalism—an international trade which under actual conditions is essentially an exchange between capitalistic and non-capitalistic modes of production (1963, p. 359).

According to Luxemburg the ways in which this process is manifested lead to the destruction of pre-capitalist modes of production, which means that realization becomes impossible and hence the reproduction of capital.

The rationale of Amin's concept of primitive accumulation shows a theoretical awareness of certain problems that are ignored by other underdevelopment theorists, but the solution he proposes is unsatisfactory. He criticizes Luxemburg's argument that capitalism requires a 'third market' (that of pre-capitalist formations) for the realization of the surplus-value contained in commodities which cannot be sold within the capitalist market to capitalists and workers (1976, p. 85), while approving her proposition that 'centre-periphery relations' depend on mechanisms of primitive accumulation rather than those of the internal laws of the capitalist mode of production (*ibid* p. 143). However, there is a trick involved here as primitive accumulation means unequal exchange, moreover the unequal exchange of commodities produced *under capitalist conditions*. 'The characteristic feature of primitive accumulation, in contrast to *normal* expanded reproduction, is unequal exchange, that is, the exchange of products whose prices of production in the Marxian sense are unequal' (p. 187, emphasis added). At the same time he asserts that the bulk of the export commodities of the Third World countries are produced under 'ultra-modern' conditions, employing the same levels of capitalization and productivity of labour as obtain in the advanced capitalist countries (p. 143, where he states that this applies to at least three-quarters of Third World exports; no evidence for these assertions is produced). The authority of Preobrazhensky (1965) is invoked to support this conception of primitive accumulation, but for Preobrazhensky, who produced the most thorough analysis of primitive accumulation after Marx, its defining feature is 'accumulation from *outside the range of capitalist production*' (1965, p. 85, emphasis added).

While Amin is certainly correct to avoid any formulation of an 'automatic collapse' theory of capitalism, it is wrong in Marxist terms to reduce its contradictions to that of realization—capacity to produce/capacity to consume—as fundamental, which comes back to the position of Rosa Luxemburg. In a recent article (1977) Amin seems to abandon the position (unique among underdevelopment theorists) of the importance of the extended reproduction of capital based on production within the advanced capitalist countries. 'It should be evident that the relatively high rates of growth in the center over the past century have been very substantially fostered by imperialist plunder' (p. 28). At the same time his claims for the theory of unequal exchange are put more modestly—' "unequal" exchange is nothing more than the mechanism of surplus-value circulation in the imperialist stage of capitalism' (p. 33). However, 'unequal exchange' in the sense of prices of production established by the equalization of the rate of profit, which serves to distribute total surplus-value in proportion to the investment of individual capitals, is a general consequence of the laws of the capitalist mode of production. It is thus applicable to relations between *all* enterprises and branches of production and so it cannot be the distinguishing feature of 'centre-periphery relations'. The unacceptability of unequal exchange as the definitive mode of exploitation under imperialism 'is the only domain in which Social Democrats, revisionists, Trotskyists, and many "leftists" (in the West) are almost unanimous in indignantly rejecting any discussion' (p. 33). This hardly squares with the extensive discussions of unequal exchange theory that have taken place, so what Amin is really complaining about is the fact that others don't agree with him, a problem resolved by vulgar name-calling.

21. The problematization of the capitalist state as an object of Marxist theory has been the area of a lively debate in recent years, stimulated in particular by the work of Nicos Poulantzas.

22. See note 31 below.

23. The impossibility of capitalist development in the periphery is expressed in teleological terms as a 'blocked transition' by Samir Amin. The article by Bill Warren which suggests that 'the prospects for successful capitalist economic development (implying industrialization) of a significant number of major underdeveloped countries are quite good' (1973, p. 3 and *passim*), unleashed a controversy bordering on hysteria, which was to be expected. Unfortunately, Warren is his own worst enemy. He accepts the postulates of underdevelopment theory as an accurate account of a previous period of capitalism in order to polemicize against them in relation to the present period. He remains within the same problematic, trying to prove empirically the possibility of capitalist development in the Third World as *national* development, free of ties of 'dependence'. His method is counterfactual, then jumps from 'empirical observations' to theoretical and political conclusions of strategic importance. The effect is once again to divert attention from the analysis of the kinds of capitalist development that *are* taking place, and their implications, to the ideological debate around 'dependence' and 'autonomy'.

24. Regarding the *static* notion of capital, the comments of Friedman (1976, p. 4) are appropriate.

Every change in the real situation tends to come as a surprise unless we are theoretically prepared for it. Such situations, where theory and reality contradict one another, ought to lead us as quickly as possible to the reconstitution of theory. Instead, it has most often led to a hardening of positions—usually reified by differing political standpoints. This in itself may help to distort attempts at explanation in such a way that we are sure to limit the relevance of our theories to particular historical situations that have become eternalized as the definition of the highest stage of or of just plain capitalism in general.

On this crucial issue see also Bradby (1975) who in her discussion of Rosa Luxemburg's theory of imperialism distinguishes 'strong theses' and 'weak theses'. The former refer to arguments that are claimed to be given in the theory of the capitalist mode of production itself, e.g. Luxemburg's view of the impossibility of realization within capitalist relations; the latter refer to the dynamics and effects of capitalist development in specified historical conditions, e.g. Luxemburg's analysis of the geographical expansion of capitalism in the search for the material elements of constant capital. What this distinction suggests is the relation of the categories of the general theory of the capitalist mode of production to the production of a theoretically specified history of capital.

It may be noted that for many underdevelopment theorists the metaphors of 'exploitation' employed reflect an obsession with primitive accumulation (in Marx's sense, 1976, Part 8), typically expressed in the vocabulary of 'pillage' and 'plunder'. For Marx these terms indicated modes of appropriation of wealth (including straightforward robbery) which contributed to the primary accumulation of capital in the transition from feudal to capitalist economy. They are not adequate to the modes of appropriation of surplus-labour through forms and relations of production subsequently established (directly or indirectly) by capital. The substitution of an abhorrence of the methods and effects of capitalist development for the work of their investigation accounts both for the moralism of much of underdevelopment theory *and* its tendency to bestow an 'essential' continuity on the history of capital (as the history of 'exploitation').

Although not free of problems (which work is?) Mandel's *Late Capitalism* (1975) is the best attempt to date to apply the means of a theoretically specified history of capitalism (Chs. 1 to 4 set out the categories employed and summarize the method and results of their application). Ironically, Mandel's *conclusions* on underdevelopment (Ch. 11 on neo-colonialism and unequal exchange) are virtually identical with those of Frank, Amin *et al* but at least they are arrived at by a very different *method* which incorporates theoretical issues quite unknown to underdevelopment theory, for example:

'the fundamental aim of the present work is to provide an explanation of the history of the capitalist mode of production in the 20th century, capable of mediating the laws of motion of "capital in general" with the concrete phenomenal forms of "many capitals". All attempts, either to confine analysis merely to the latter, or to deduce them directly from the former, are without methodological justification or hope of practical success. (pp. 8–9). The cyclical course of the capitalist mode of production induced by competition takes the form of the successive expansion and contraction of commodity production and hence of the production of surplus-value. There corresponds to this a further cyclical movement of expansion and contraction in the realization of surplus-value and the accumulation of capital. In their timing, their volume and their proportions, the realization of surplus-value and the accumulation of capital are neither wholly identical with each other nor with the production of surplus-value itself' (p.108).

25. 'It is useful to retain the positive value placed on the term *development*, and to formulate the proposition that *development is first of all the development of man out of conditions of exploitation, poverty and oppression* . . . (The second proposition) is that *development always involves changes in the basic institutions and structures of society* . . . Not all structural changes, however, are necessarily developmental when development is seen from the humanist perspective that focuses upon the situation of man . . . *Development is the happy coincidence of structural change and improvement in the human condition*' (Johnson, 1972b, pp. 272–3).

26. Foster-Carter's celebration of 'neo-Marxism' has been completely demolished by John Taylor's criticism (1974).

27. Labour-power 'can appear on the market as a commodity only if, and in so far as, its possessor, the individual whose labour-power it is, offers it for sale or sells it as a commodity. In order that its possessor may sell it as a commodity, he must have it at his disposal, he must be the free proprietor of his own labour-capacity, hence of his person' (Marx, 1976, p. 271). For Engels the solution of the problem of surplus-value, involving the theorization of labour-power as a commodity, was 'the most epoch-making achievement of Marx's work' (1936, p. 228)—but not for Immanuel Wallerstein, obviously.

The fascination with colonial plantation economies based on unfree labour as 'paradigmatic' of capitalist exploitation is also evident in the work of Frank (e.g. 1972a, Ch. 1)—see also note 24 above.

28. Not only does this statement employ multiple criteria of 'social stratification' in the characteristic manner of sociology (income, status, ethnicity etc.), but its innocence of any concept of social relations of production might puzzle the reader as to where the

'surplus' of the notorious 'surplus drain' comes from. For similarly sociologistic presentations of 'social class' see Johnson, 1972b; Shivji, 1975.

29. 'Real *development* involves a structural transformation of the economy, society and polity and culture of the satellite that permits the self-generating and self-perpetuating use and development of the people's potential. Development comes about as a consequence of a people's frontal attack on the oppression, exploitation, and poverty that they suffer at the hands of the dominant classes and their system' (Cockcroft, Frank and Johnson, 1972, p. xvi).

O'Brien (1975, p. 25) has shrewdly observed that 'Much writing on dependency seems to leave one with the vision of the desirability of an anti-imperialist, populist leader uniting his people under a technocratic state'. See further note 31.

30. Leys (1977), from the Left, and Dore (1976), from the Right, have both commented on the appeal of underdevelopment theory to the 'unhappy consciousness' (Leys) or 'white man's guilt' (Dore) of Western intellectuals.

31. Lenin's writings in opposition to the positions of the Narodniks (1960 IIa, 1960 IIb, 1960 III) provide a critical analysis, unparalleled in its force and precision, of the combination of moralism and theoretical errors in the analysis of capitalism, and their effects in concrete analysis and in politics. One of the features of Narodnism which Lenin drew attention to was its 'bureaucratic mentality' (1960 IIb, p. 523) as reflecting a certain view of the privileged status of the intelligentsia in its relations with the state. Something of this is glimpsed in the notion of *policies of underdevelopment* in Frank (1972a) and of *policies of primitive accumulation* in Amin (1967), which links to the observation of Leys that 'socialist revolution' functions as a utopian and populist vehicle (that is, incapable of specification in terms of the conditions, forms of organization and strategies of class struggle). A vehicle of what?—one that will carry the intelligentsia into a position where it can formulate *policies of 'development'*. The conditions of enlightened voluntarism thus established, the strategy of 'development' 'must radically revise the capitalist model of resource allocation and reject the rules of profitability', and must embody 'a radical revision of economic choices' (Amin, 1976, pp. 383, 384). This perspective, populist in form and technocratic in content, is further exemplified in Thomas, 1974 (see also the comments on Amin by Disney, 1977). Sutcliffe (1972) and O'Brien (1975) have noted the relevance of the classic Russian Marxist debates on the development of capitalism to current discussions of underdevelopment. A fuller treatment of the lessons that the latter could learn from the former would be valuable.

REFERENCES

Abdel-Malek, A., 1967, 'Sociologie du développement national: problèmes de conceptualization', *Revue de l'Institut de Sociologie*, No. 2/3.

Alavi, H., 1972, 'The state in post-colonial societies: Pakistan and Bangladesh', *New Left Review* No. 74.

Alavi, H., 1975, 'India and the colonial mode of production', in the *Socialist Register 1975* ed. R. Miliband and J. Saville, London.

Amin, S., 1973, *L'échange inégal et la loi de valeur*, Paris.

Amin, S., 1974a, *Accumulation on a World Scale*, 2 vols., New York and London.

Amin, S., 1974b, 'Le capitalisme et la rente foncière' in *La question paysanne et le capitalisme* by Amin and K. Vergopoulos, Paris.

Amin, S., 1974c, 'Accumulation and development: a theoretical model', *Review of African Political Economy* No. 1.

Amin, S., 1976, *Unequal Development*, Hassocks, Sussex.

Amin, S., 1976a, *L'imperialisme et le développement inégal*, Paris.

Amin, S., 1977, 'Capitalism, state collectivism and socialism', *Monthly Review* Vol. 29 No. 2.

Aron, R., 1964, *Industrial Society*, London.

Arrighi, G., 1971,' The relationship between the colonial and the class structures: a critique of A. G. Frank's theory of "the development of underdevelopment" ', IDEP Dakar, mimeo.

Banaji, J., 1972, 'For a theory of colonial modes of production', *Economic and Political Weekly*, Vol. 7 No. 52.

Banaji, J., 1975a, 'Modes of production in a materialist conception of history', Dar es Salaam, mimeo.

Banaji, J., 1975b, 'Comment on India and the colonial mode of production', *Economic and Political Weekly*, Vol. 10 No. 49. reply to Alavi

Banaji, R., 1976, 'Prelude to a critique of Samir Amin', Dar es Salaam, mimeo.

Baran, P., 1957, *The Political Economy of Growth*, New York.

Baran, P., and P. Sweezy, 1966, *Monopoly Capital*, New York.

Beckford, G., 1969, 'The economics of agricultural resource use and development in plantation economies', *Social and Economic Studies*, Vol. 18.

Beckford, G., 1972, *Persistent Poverty*, New York.

Bendix, R., 1967, 'Tradition and modernity reconsidered', *Comparative Studies in Society and History*, Vol. 9 No. 3.

Bernstein, H., 1971, 'Modernization theory and the sociological study of development', *Journal of Development Studies*, Vol. 7 No. 2.

Bernstein, H., 1972, 'Breakdowns of modernization', *Journal of Development Studies*, Vol. 8 No. 2.

Bernstein, H., 1977, 'Marxism and African history: Endre Sik and his critics', *Kenyan Historical Review* Vol. 5 No. 1.

Bernstein, H., and Pitt, M., 1974, 'Plantations and modes of exploitation', *Journal of Peasant Studies* Vol. 1 No. 4.

Bernstein, H., and Depelchin, J., 1978, 'The object of African history. A materialist perspective', *History in Africa* Vol. 5.

Blumer, H., 1966, 'The idea of social development', *Studies in Comparative International Development* Vol. 2 No. 1.

Booth, D., 1975, 'André Gunder Frank: an introduction and appreciation', in Oxaal, Barnett and Booth ed.

Bradby, B., 1975, 'The destruction of natural economy', *Economy and Society*, Vol. 4 No. 2.

Cardoso, F. H., 1972, 'Dependency and development in Latin America', *New Left Review* No. 74.

Chodak, S., 1973, *Societal Development*, New York.

Chomsky, N., 1969, *American Power and the New Mandarins*, Harmondsworth.

Cockcroft, J. D., Frank, A. G., and Johnson, D. L., 1972, *Dependence and Underdevelopment*, New York.

Cruise O'Brien, D., 1972, 'Modernization, order and the erosion of a democratic ideal: American political science, 1969–70', *Journal of Development Studies* Vol. 8 No. 3.

Culley, L., 1977, 'The State and Economic Development in pro-Marxist theory', paper presented to the annual conference of the British Sociological Association.

de Kadt, E., 1974, 'Introduction' to *Sociology and Development* ed. de Kadt and G. Williams, London.

Disney, N., 1977, 'Accumulation on a World Scale', *The Insurgent Sociologist* Vol. 7 No. 2.

Dore, R. P., 1976, 'Editorial' in *IDS Bulletin* Vol. 8 No. 2, special issue on 'Culture Revisited'.

Dos Santos, T., 1973, 'The crisis of development theory and the problem of dependence in Latin America' in *Underdevelopment and Development*, ed. H. Bernstein, Harmondsworth.

Eisenstadt, S. N., 1966, *Modernization: Protest and Change*, Englewood Cliffs, N. J.

Eisenstadt, S. N., 1969, 'Breakdowns of modernization' in *Readings in Social Evolution and Development* ed. Eisenstadt, London.

Eisenstadt, S. N., ed., 1968, *The Protestant Ethic and Modernization*, New York.

Emmanuel, A., 1972, *Unequal Exchange*, London.

Emmanuel, A., 1975, 'Unequal exchange revisited', Discussion Paper No. 77, Institute of Development Studies, Sussex.

Engels, F., 1936, *Anti-Dühring*, London.

Ennew, J., Hirst, P., and Tribe, K., 1977, ' "Peasantry" as an economic category', *Journal of Peasant Studies*, Vol. 4 No. 4.

Foster-Carter, A., 1974, 'Neo-Marxist approaches to development and underdevelopment', in *Sociology and Development*, ed. E. de Kadt and G. Williams, London.

Frank, A. G., 1966, 'The development of underdevelopment', *Monthly Review*, Vol. 18 No. 4.

Frank, A. G., 1967, 'Sociology of development and underdevelopment of sociology', *Catalyst* No. 3.

Frank, A. G., 1969a, *Capitalism and Underdevelopment in Latin America*, New York and London.

Frank, A. G., 1969b, *Latin America. Underdevelopment or Revolution*, New York and London.

Frank, A. G., 1972a, *Lumpenbourgeoisie: Lumpendevelopment*, New York and London.

Frank, A. G., 1972b, 'Economic dependence, class structure and underdevelopment policy', in Cockcroft, Frank and Johnson.

Friedman, J., 1976, 'Crises in theory and transformations of the world economy', Centre for Development Research, Copenhagen, mimeo.

Furtado, C., 1964, *Development and Underdevelopment*, Berkeley, Cal.

Gerstein, I., 1977, 'Theories of the world economy and imperialism', *The Insurgent Sociologist* Vol. 7 No. 2.

Godelier, M., 1974, 'On the definition of a social formation', *Critique of Anthropology* No. 1.   on m.ps

Hilal, J., 1970, 'Sociology and underdevelopment', University of Durham, mimeo.

Hirst, P. Q., 1976, *Social Evolution and Sociological Categories,* London.

Hoogvelt, A. M., 1976, *The Sociology of Developing Societies,* London.

Hopkins, A. G., 1975, 'On importing André Gunder Frank into Africa', *African Economic History Review* Vol. 2 No. 1.

Hoselitz, B. F., 1963, 'Main concepts in the analysis of the implications of technological change' in *Industrialization and Society* ed. Hoselitz and W. E. Moore, Paris.

Hoselitz, B. F., 1965, 'The use of historical comparisons in the study of economic development', in *Social Development* ed. R. Aron and Hoselitz, Paris.

Hoselitz, B. F., ed., 1952, *The Progress of Underdeveloped Areas*, Chicago.

Johnson, D. L., 1972a, 'Dependence and the international system', in Cockcroft, Frank and Johnson.

Johnson, D. L., 1972b, 'On oppressed classes', in Cockcroft, Frank and Johnson.

Journal of Development Studies, 1972, Vol. 9 No. 1, special issue on 'Science and Technology in Development'.

Kay, G., 1975, *Development and Underdevelopment*, London.

Kerr, C. *et al., Industrialism and Industrial Man,* New York.

Laclau, E., 1971, 'Feudalism and capitalism in Latin America', *New Left Review* No. 67.

Lamb, R. K., 1952, 'Political elites and the process of economic development', in Hoselitz ed.

Lenin, V. I., 1960 IIa, 'A characterization of economic romanticism', *Collected Works,* Moscow, Vol. II.

Lenin, V. I., 1960 IIb, 'The heritage we renounce', *Collected Works,* vol. II.

Lenin, V. I., 1960 III, *The Development of Capitalism in Russia, Collected Works,* Vol. III.

Lerner, D., 1958, *The Passing of Traditional Society,* New York.

Lerner, D., 1967, 'Comparative analysis of processes of modernization', in *The City in Modern Africa* ed. H. Miner, London.

Levin, J. V., 1960, *The Export Economies,* Cambridge, Mass.

Leys, C., 1977, 'Underdevelopment and dependency: critical notes', *Journal of Contemporary Asia* Vol. 7 No. 1.

Littlejohn, G., 1977, 'Chayanov and the theory of peasant economy' in *Sociological Theories of the Economy* ed. B. Hindess, London.

Long, N., 1975, 'Structural dependency, modes of production and economic brokerage in Peru', in Oxaal, Barnett and Booth ed.

Long, N., 1977, *An Introduction to the Sociology of Rural Development,* London.

Luxemburg, R., 1963, *The Accumulation of Capital,* London.

Magdoff, H., 1972, 'Imperialism without colonies' in *Studies in the Theory of Imperialism,* ed. R. Owen and B. Sutcliffe, London.

Mandel, E., 1975, *Late Capitalism,* London.

Marx, K., 1976, *Capital* Vol. I, Harmondsworth.

McClelland, D., 1961, *The Achieving Society,* New York.

McClelland, D., 1964, 'Business drive and national achievement', in *Social Change* ed. A. Etzioni and E. Etzioni, New York.

Meillassoux, C., 1975, *Femmes, greniers et capitaux,* Paris.

Moore, W. E., 1963a, *Social Change,* Englewood Cliffs, N. J.

Moore, W. E., 1963b, 'Introduction. Social change and comparative studies', *International Social Science Journal* Vol. 15 No. 4, special issue on 'The Sociology of Development in Latin America'.

Morse, C., *et al,* 1969, *Modernization by Design,* Ithaca and London.

Myint, H., 1958, 'An interpretation of economic backwardness', in *The Economics of Underdevelopment* ed. A. N. Agarwala and A. P. Singh, New York.

Nettl, J. P., 1967, *Political Mobilization,* London.

Nisbet, R. A., 1969, *Social Change and History,* New York.

Nove, A., 1974, 'On reading André Gunder Frank', *Journal of Development Studies,* Vol. 10 No. 3/4.

Nurkse, R. 1953, *Problems of Capital Formation in Underdeveloped Countries*, Oxford.
O'Brien, P., 1975, 'A critique of Latin American theories of dependency', in Oxaal, Barnett and Booth ed.
Oxaal, I., Barnett, A., and Booth, D., ed., 1975, *Beyond the Sociology of Development*, London.
Parsons, T., 1966, *Societies. Evolutionary and Comparative Perspectives*, Englewood Cliffs, N. J.
Phillips, A., 1977, 'The concept of development', *Review of African Political Economy* No. 8.
Pilling, G., 1973, 'Imperialism, trade and "unequal exchange": the work of Aghiri Emmanuel', *Economy and Society* Vol. 2 No. 2.
Preobrazhensky, E., 1965, *The New Economics*, London.
Rey, P.-Ph., 1973, *Les alliances de classes*, Paris.
Rey, P.-Ph., 1976, *Capitalisme négrier*, Paris.
Rhodes, R. I., 1969, 'The disguised conservatism in evolutionary development theory', *Science and Society* Vol. 32 No. 3.
Rodney, W., 1972, *How Europe Underdeveloped Africa*, Dar es Salaam and London.
Rostow, W. W., 1960, *The Stages of Economic Growth*, London.
Seers, D., 1969, 'The meaning of development', *International Development Review*, Vol. 11.
Shivji, I. G., 1975, *Class Struggles in Tanzania*, Dar es Salaam and London.
Sik, E., 1966 and 1974, *The History of Black Africa*, 4 vols., Budapest.
Singer, H. W., and Ansari, J., 1977, *Rich Countries and Poor Countries*, London.
Smelser, N. J., 1963, 'Mechanisms of change and adjustment to change', in *Industrialization and Society* ed. Hoselitz and Moore, Paris.
Smelser, N. J., 1968, 'Toward a general theory of social change', in his *Essays in Sociological Explanation*, Englewood Cliffs, N. J.
Smelser, N. J., and Lipset, S. M., 1968, 'Social structure, mobility and economic development' in Smelser, *Essays in Sociological Explanation*.
Sutcliffe, B., 1972, 'Conclusion' in *Studies in the Theory of Imperialism* ed. Owen and Sutcliffe, London.
Taylor, J., 1974, 'Neo-Marxism and underdevelopment—a sociological phantasy', *Journal of Contemporary Asia*, Vol. 4 No. 1.
Terray, E., 1972, *Marxism and 'Primitive' Societies*, New York and London.
Thomas, C., 1974, *Dependence and Transformation*, New York and London.
Thorner, D., Kerblay, B., Smith, R. E. F., ed., 1966, A. V. Chayanov: *The Theory of Peasant Economy*, Homewood, Ill.
Tschannerl, G., 1976, 'Periphery capitalist development—a case study of the Tanzanian economy', *Utafiti* Vol. 1 No. 1.
Tribe, K., 1976, 'Economic property and commodity exchange in the formation of agrarian capitalism', paper presented to Peasants Seminar, Centre of International and Area Studies, University of London.
Von Freyhold, M., n.d., 'The rise and fall of colonial modes of production' Dar es Salaam, mimeo.
Wallerstein, I., 1974a, *The Modern World System*, New York.
Wallerstein, I., 1974b, 'The rise and future demise of the world capitalist system: concepts for comparative analysis', *Comparative Studies in Society and History*, Vol. 16.
Warren, B., 1973, 'Imperialism and capitalist industrialization', *New Left Review* No. 81.
Weber, M., 1930, *The Protestant Ethic and the Spirit of Capitalism*, London.
Weinberg, I., 1969, 'The problem of the convergence of industrial societies: a critical look at the state of a theory', *Comparative Studies in Society and History* Vol. 11 No. 1.
Weiner, M., ed., 1966, *Modernization*, New York.
Wuyts, M., 1976, 'On the nature of underdevelopment: an analysis of two views of underdevelopment', Dar es Salaam, mimeo.